David Morris

Scrum

In easy steps is an imprint of In Easy Steps Limited
16 Hamilton Terrace · Holly Walk · Leamington Spa
Warwickshire · United Kingdom · CV32 4LY
www.ineasysteps.com

Notice of Liability
Every effort has been made to ensure that this book contains accurate
and current information. However, In Easy Steps Limited and the
authors shall not be liable for any loss or damage suffered by readers
as a result of any information contained herein.

Trademarks
All trademarks are acknowledged as belonging to their respective
companies.

In Easy Steps Limited supports The Forest Stewardship Council (FSC),
the leading international forest certification organisation. All our titles
that are printed on Greenpeace approved FSC certified paper carry the
FSC logo.

MIX
Paper from
responsible sources
FSC® C020837

Printed and bound in the United Kingdom

ISBN 978-1-84078-731-3

Contents

1 Introducing Scrum

This chapter explains how developing novel products for complex markets requires an iterative design and incremental development approach, like Scrum.

Introduction

This book is intended for anyone interested in understanding the Scrum framework for agile product development. It serves as an introduction to those forming or joining their first Scrum Team. It provides a useful compendium of techniques to use at each stage of product Discovery and Delivery. And finally, it acts as a reference for anyone who needs to interact with Scrum Teams.

The use of agile approaches for product development continues to evolve as organizations face uncertainty and disruption. Scrum is the most widely adopted agile framework, often together with other methods, such as Extreme Programming (see page 105).

Learning Scrum in stages

As you begin using Scrum, you will go through development stages, often described using the martial arts term *Shu-Ha-Ri*:

- **Shu** (follow the rules): during the first stage of adoption, teams should stick to the basic techniques and rules of Scrum; this book is an essential companion to that journey.

- **Ha** (break the rules): in the second stage, teams rise above the basics to work together and drive organization change; Chapters Nine and Ten focus on how teams continually improve.

- **Ri** (form new rules): finally, teams who have mastered Scrum will typically require little outside guidance, such as provided by this book, and instead become role models for other teams.

Learning Scrum in easy steps

The In Easy Steps series of books is designed to take readers step-by-step through new topics, learning through the experience of doing, rather than forcing readers to work their way through pages of theory and being left to find their own way.

The best way to learn Scrum is to be in a Scrum Team and to experience it first-hand. For those who want to understand Scrum but are not yet in a team, the next best way is to see it play out step-by-step. **Scrum in easy steps** guides you through forming a team and then taking them through the whole product development life-cycle, from Discovery to Delivery and beyond.

To illustrate this, as you work your way through the book you will also be following the experience of a pizza takeaway business – called Dante's – who want to start taking orders online.

守破離

All pages that include an example from Dante's, the pizza takeaway used for illustration, will be highlighted with this pizza slice in the margin.

About Scrum in easy steps

This first chapter shows how the Scrum framework will help you to cope in today's challenging environment. Chapters Two through to Ten walk through Scrum, step-by-step.

For those looking for a **quick reference** to the whole Scrum framework, start with Chapter Eleven.

Forming your first Scrum Team
One of the biggest shifts you will face when adopting Scrum is how people work together and the changes in role this requires. Chapter Two discusses the three key roles in Scrum: Product Owner, Scrum Master, and the Delivery Team.

Discovering the product
A key factor in successfully delivering great products is to prepare a good breakdown of the work required. Chapters Three to Five cover how Product Owners work with others to discover, define, and plan delivery of the product through the Product Backlog.

Delivering the product
The next three chapters step through the typical development cycle (the Sprint), detailing the events, artifacts, and techniques used. Chapter Six covers how a Sprint starts with the Delivery Team agreeing a Sprint goal, and the work required to achieve it.

Chapter Seven covers the typical daily routine of the team as they design, build, and test the product, tracking progress, handling impediments, and re-planning to achieve their Sprint goal.

Chapter Eight shows how the team reviews their completed work with their stakeholders and gets feedback on what should be their next priorities for the Product Backlog.

Continually improving and scaling Scrum
Just as teams review the product each Sprint, they also need to consider their approach. Chapter Nine explores how Scrum Masters work with the team to continually improve – while Chapter Ten deals with how they support the organization getting better at Scrum, especially at working with multiple teams.

The Scrum reference
The final chapter wraps up by providing a quick reference of the whole Scrum framework, the roles, the events, the artifacts, and the rules that explain how they interact and work together.

Why development is hard

Identifying a new product that will solve a problem, and getting it right first time is full of complexity, uncertainty, and risk. There is no single correct approach that will guarantee success.

When you are developing novel products in a new and growing market, there is much that remains unknown. You need to get feedback from potential customers as fast as possible, and follow an approach that allows you to improve and re-release the product as you learn more about what works.

As markets mature, however, the product becomes more defined and uncertainty reduces, at which point you will require a more scalable reliable approach. Should the product ever reach the point of becoming a commodity, you will then tend to focus more on reducing cost by making your processes as simple as possible.

Knowing what product you are developing and what market you are targeting will help guide your product development approach.

Understanding your product

The **Pace-Layered Application Strategy** was developed to help us choose the right approach to managing our products.

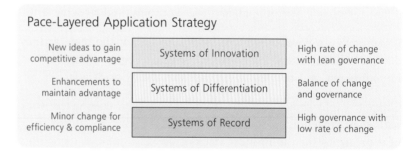

Pace-Layered Application Strategy

New ideas to gain competitive advantage	Systems of Innovation	High rate of change with lean governance
Enhancements to maintain advantage	Systems of Differentiation	Balance of change and governance
Minor change for efficiency & compliance	Systems of Record	High governance with low rate of change

- **Systems of Innovation** are creative responses to new opportunities, and typically require an experimental approach that generates feedback or results quickly.

- **Systems of Differentiation** create a unique selling point for an existing market or product, and require careful thought combined with fast implementation.

- **Systems of Record** handle mission-critical administration and transactions and require standardized processes, operational efficiency, and compliance with governance.

Don't forget

The *Pace-Layered Application Strategy* was developed as a decision support framework by Gartner Inc.

10

Understanding your market

The **Cynefin Framework** was developed to help us make sense of our situation and choose the right approach to managing change.

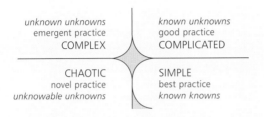

Don't forget

The *Cynefin Framework* was developed as a decision support framework by Dave Snowden. *Cynefin* is a Welsh word meaning habitats or domains.

- In **simple** situations, the connection between cause and effect is clear, and from that the course of action will be obvious – suiting a simpler checklist approach.

- In **complicated** situations, the link between cause and effect has to be uncovered, through expert analysis, to decide the right response – suiting a more thorough plan-driven process.

- In **complex** situations, there are no direct connections between cause and effect – we need to feel our way one step at a time – suiting a more exploratory feedback-driven process.

- Finally, in **chaotic** situations, we need to stabilize our organization urgently – suiting immediate action – typically not a safe place for product development.

The right approach for your product in your market

Once you have understood your product type and the dynamics of your market, you can select an approach that is best suited to discovering and delivering your product. If the answer involves innovation and complexity, then a checklist or plan-driven approach is not suitable. Scrum is an ideal framework to follow.

However, even if you follow a plan-driven approach for most of your projects, you will find that you will benefit from adopting a feedback-driven approach some of the time.

While Dante's, our pizza company, is in an established market, they are unfamiliar with online ordering. They adopted Scrum so they get fast feedback, learn what works, and improve rapidly.

The use of the term *Scrum* originated from this 1986 article in the Harvard Business Review.

A feedback-driven approach

The shift from a plan-driven to a feedback-driven approach to product development also requires a shift in mindset:

> "The traditional sequential *relay race* approach to product development – exemplified by phased program planning – may conflict with the goals of maximum speed and flexibility. Instead, a holistic or *rugby* approach – where a team tries to go the distance as a unit, passing the ball back and forth – may better serve today's competitive requirements."
> *Harvard Business Review*

Plan-driven product development

The plan-driven approach to product development starts by defining exactly what the product should do. This scope is signed off as a specification. The team then carries out further work to analyze, then design, then build, and then test a product they believe meets that specification. Finally, they present the finished product which may or may not be accepted as meeting the specification. This approach suits simpler products in stable markets where the requirements are unlikely to change and the technical solution is well-known.

Feedback-driven product development

The feedback-driven approach to product development starts out with an expectation that scope will evolve and change as the product is progressively developed. Instead, we fix the size of the team and the amount of time we are willing to invest in delivering as many as possible of the prioritized features the customer wants. This approach suits novel products in emerging markets where the requirements cannot be fully known up front, or where the technology is still evolving.

The difference between the two approaches is illustrated below:

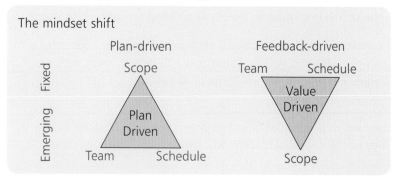

The mindset shift

To be effective, this shift also requires some new practices that enable teams to develop with speed, flexibility and feedback:

The self-organizing autonomous team

Teams should be free to determine the best technology, architecture, and approach to developing the product. They should think of themselves like a start-up, taking initiative and defining their own identity. To support and enable this level of autonomy, there should also be clear expectations and enough checkpoints to avoid instability, tension, and chaos.

The learning team

As teams grow and discover how to solve their problems, they will experience a range of learning across levels (e.g. individuals, the team, and the wider organization) and across functions (e.g. analysis, programming, and quality assurance). It is vital that this learning is encouraged and that opportunities are also found to transfer this to people outside the team.

Overlapping development stages

The team should work together across all activities, testing one feature while they are building a second feature, at the same time as they are planning a third. This is in contrast to the plan-driven approach that makes a team wait for all requirements to be specified in a plan before starting the build, for all build work to be completed before starting any testing, and for all testing to be completed before anything can be reviewed.

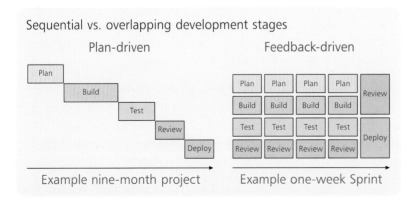

Sequential vs. overlapping development stages

This enables them to re-plan or do further build work immediately, when required, rather than waiting for a new project.

Iterative and incremental

As we explored feedback-driven approaches to product development, we found a blend of approaches more appropriate.

Cycling back through stages

One of the simplest ideas for incorporating feedback is to repeat as necessary the stages of analysis, design, programming, testing, and integration. Teams should actively pursue feedback from their stakeholders as they go, and if they find they have misunderstood anything, cycle back to the appropriate earlier stage to fix it. However, while this encourages use of feedback, it treats it as an exception rather than something that can be anticipated.

Iterative design

Iterative design is a deliberately cyclical process of prototyping, testing, analyzing, and refining a product design. Changes are made to the most recent iteration of a design, based on feedback. With iterative design, feedback is encouraged, and repeating the whole cycle is assumed.

In early cycles, there is a greater concentration on analysis and design with a little programming to generate feedback. As work progresses, understanding of the product will stabilize, so that instead of reworking the analysis or design, more time is dedicated to programming and testing.

Incremental development

Incremental development is a progressive process where the product is built a feature at a time (designed, built, and tested incrementally) until it is finished. In effect, the product is broken down into its component features, each of which is developed and delivered separately. This allows the earlier release of some features which should speed up return on investment.

Iterative design with incremental development

In order for product development to be truly feedback-driven, it is essential that the product is released progressively and repeatedly. Each release should be complete and usable, each one adding more functionality, until the product is complete.

For this to be effective, you need to prioritize features so that the most useful and valuable ones are developed first. Features must be decomposed into small increments that can be delivered separately.

The Scrum framework

Scrum is a feedback-driven framework for product development that incorporates iterative design, incremental development, self-organizing teams, and continual improvement.

The Scrum Team

There are three key roles within the team:

- **Product Owner**: responsible for the business value of the product, selecting *what* gets done and explaining *why*.

- **Delivery Team**: the programmers, testers, analysts, etc. who self-organize to decide *how* the work gets done, and do it.

- **Scrum Master**: responsible for ensuring the team is motivated, productive, and following their working agreement.

Events in Scrum

There are five events central to the Scrum framework:

- **Sprint**: the block of time within which all work and the events below take place – most often two weeks.

- **Sprint Planning**: in which the team agrees with the Product Owner the functionality to be developed in a Sprint, and then plan the work they need to do in order to deliver it.

- **Daily Scrum**: in which the team look at their progress, the work remaining, any impediments, and re-plan as required.

- **Sprint Review**: in which the team share the progress they have made with their stakeholders and elicit their feedback.

- **Sprint Retrospective**: in which the team consider how well the last Sprint went, and agree possible improvement actions.

Artifacts of Scrum

There are three core artifacts:

- **Product Backlog**: a prioritized breakdown of the work required to build the desired product.

- **Sprint Backlog**: a sub-set of items from the Product Backlog that the team agrees to complete in a single Sprint, with Tasks.

- **Product Increment**: the product features completed within a Sprint, built on top of product features already released.

Don't forget

The Product Increment should be released at the end of each Sprint. However, Product Owners often choose to wait. For this reason, this is often described as a Potentially Shippable Increment (PSI).

Summary

- Developing novel products in complex markets is a risky and costly business. It is difficult to plan and then build everything a customer might need or that might delight them.

- The development and support approach to use will depend on the type of product: while established and regulated products might suit a more plan-driven approach, more novel products suit a more exploratory feedback-driven approach.

- The type of market will also drive the choice of an appropriate development and support approach: stable mature markets might suit a high-volume simple approach, while newer emerging markets suit a more feedback-driven approach.

- With feedback-driven development, focus shifts more to fixing the time and resources, and flexing the scope based on early and ongoing feedback.

- A feedback-driven approach requires overlapping the development stages of analysis, build, and testing – by enabling these to happen at the same time, teams can respond more quickly to changing requirements.

- Feedback-driven development requires self-organizing teams who are able to reflect on their progress and learn as they go.

- Iterative design allows a product to be progressively defined as the team gets feedback and learns more.

- Incremental development allows the product to grow by adding and releasing features progressively.

- A feedback-driven approach benefits most from combining both iterative design and incremental development, as this allows new requirements to be discovered and progressively added to the product.

- Scrum is a feedback-driven product development framework that combines iterative design and incremental development, based on self-organizing learning teams.

- Like learning anything new, becoming proficient in Scrum goes through stages of competency – most commonly referred to using the martial arts concept of Shu Ha Ri.

2 Forming a Scrum Team

Scrum is built on teams that collaborate well. This chapter explores how the Delivery Team, Product Owner, and Scrum Master work together and with other roles outside of Scrum.

Getting started with Scrum

Adopting Scrum requires a shift in mindset – and for many organizations, an overall cultural adjustment too. It will be harder if you have to change from a plan-driven to a feedback-driven product development approach like Scrum.

However, if you fully commit to Scrum you will discover that not only are you capable of speed and flexibility, you will also unleash creativity and innovation within your teams and build even better products.

Scrum values

Scrum is underpinned by a set of values that act as the foundation for how teams work and interact:

- **Focus**: teams collaborate better and deliver more valuable items faster when they limit work-in-progress.

- **Courage**: teams can take on big challenges through a balance of holding each other to account and being supportive.

- **Openness**: teams are more effective when they can honestly express their progress and what concerns them.

- **Commitment**: teams are more committed to succeed when they can self-organize around the work to be done.

- **Respect**: teams become high-performing through developing their skills and behavior together.

Start with filling the roles in a Scrum Team

The best way to get started with Scrum is to:

1 Identify who can fulfill the roles in a Scrum Team

2 Provide initial training so they understand and buy into their responsibilities

3 Get them started as soon as possible, as teams learn best from experiment and feedback

4 Provide coaching to all the roles, progressively encourage the Scrum Master to take on that coaching, and for the team members to support and coach each other

Clear roles

As a product development framework, Scrum benefits from having only three roles. Rather than a set of formal job titles, these roles describe a set of well-defined responsibilities for discovering and delivering the product, and continually improving.

Start with the outcome in mind

Scrum is focused on being able to deliver a potentially shippable Product Increment every Sprint. This means that you should have a well-defined Product Backlog before asking a Delivery Team to start. Therefore, the best role to fill first is Product Owner. Once they are in place, they can kick off the product Discovery work (see Chapters Three to Five) while you work to fill the other roles.

Find a servant-leader

To grow an effective and high-performing Scrum Team, you need to find someone for the Scrum Master role who knows how to support and coach a team well. This requires a balance of serving the team – by ensuring a working environment free from outside interference – at the same time as leading the team – by guiding them in how to follow the Scrum framework.

Build a team of awesome

While the Product Owner is building the Product Backlog, get started with the Scrum Master to form a well-balanced Delivery Team. They will need all the skills and experience necessary to design, build, test, and release a working increment of the product every Sprint. Not all teams can be the A-team from day one, so you will also need a sound plan for team and individual coaching.

Checks and balances

Each role is distinct and vital to the Scrum Team's success. Delivery Team members are encouraged to be multi-disciplined. For example, programmers could run tests – on other people's code – and testers can write specifications. While any team member could act as Scrum Master, a dedicated person in that role is recommended for continuity and focus.

The Product Owner, on the other hand, is typically driven to get the Delivery Team to deliver more and faster, so they cannot also be a team member. As the Scrum Master helps protect the team and ensures they work at a sustainable pace, the Product Owner cannot be a Scrum Master either.

The role of Product Owner

The role of Product Owner is critical to delivering a product that will delight customers, generate a good return on investment and deliver value to your organization. The responsibilities of acting as Product Owner to a Scrum Team are significant and should be considered a full-time role rather than some additional activities that can be added onto someone's current job.

The Product Owner represents the needs of all key stakeholders, the voice of the customer and the operational needs of the enterprise. They call on all these parties to help determine what is **desirable** and **viable** for their product. They should also work very closely with their delivery and support colleagues, to ensure that they also appreciate what is **feasible**.

Product Owners typically come from a product management background, which normally means that they have responsibility for their product *from the cradle to the grave*. In larger organizations, Product Owners will often focus more on product development, while their senior colleagues will focus on the product once it has been released to the market, and also providing customer feedback.

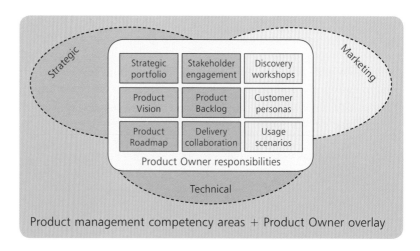

Product management competency areas + Product Owner overlay

Responsibilities of the Product Owner
Whatever their position in the product management organization, the Product Owner has to be capable of balancing the strategic and the technical – communicating a vision for their product while working with the team day-to-day – as shown on the product management competency model above.

The full responsibilities of the role of Product Owner include:

- Develop their product's Vision, Strategy, and Roadmap.

- Understand their potential customers' stated needs, as well as what would delight them.

- Work with stakeholders to capture all internal needs.

- Define the Business Value in the product.

- Work responsibly with the team to understand technical risk.

- Take ownership of their product's Release Plan.

- Measure and be accountable for the return on investment.

In Dante's, our pizza takeaway business, the owner's niece Karly will act as the Product Owner. She has experience as a business analyst, cares enough that the business will succeed, and has been released from working full-time in the business to allow for this.

Behavior patterns for Product Owners
In order to get the most from the Delivery Team, the Product Owner should typically exhibit the following behaviors:

- Be honest about the value, scope, and costs of their product.

- Be knowledgeable about the product and the business.

- Communicate directly with any stakeholder of the team.

- Ensure the Product Backlog balances value, risk, and quality.

- Lead refinement so that the Product Backlog is ready for use.

- Make the time to respond promptly to the team's questions.

- Provide feedback to help the team to improve the product.

- Ensure open and transparent communication of progress.

- Decide when the team's work is ready to be released.

- Never force the team to start work they consider not ready.

- Never tell the team how to do their work.

- Never introduce new work part-way through a Sprint.

The role of Scrum Master

The Scrum Master's role is to facilitate the work of the team. Although they are not formally a team lead, they do act as a buffer between the team and any potential outside distractions.

The Scrum Master also ensures that the team follows the Scrum framework and strives to meet their commitments. For example, it is critical that the team should not bring work into the Sprint other than through, or with the agreement of, the Product Owner.

These twin aspects of the Scrum Master's role have led to it being described as a servant-leader. They are responsible for supporting the team, the Product Owner, and the wider organization.

Coaching the Delivery Team

The Scrum Master supports the team by:

- Ensuring they have a productive work environment.

- Coaching them in self-organization and collaboration.

- Encouraging them to work with the Product Owner to refine the Product Backlog.

- Helping them to resolve anything that impedes their progress – and escalating on their behalf, where necessary.

- Facilitating Scrum events and other sessions as needed.

- Coaching them in how to follow the Scrum framework and how to apply the techniques and practices involved.

Coaching the Product Owner

The Scrum Master supports the Product Owner by:

- Ensuring they can define and prioritize the Product Backlog.

- Understanding the organization's long-term product plans.

- Assisting the team in refining the Product Backlog.

- Helping them to resolve empowerment issues – and escalating on their behalf, where necessary.

- Facilitating Scrum events and other sessions as needed.

- Coaching them in how to follow the Scrum framework and how to apply the techniques and practices involved.

Coaching the organization

The Scrum Master also supports the rest of the organization by:

- Planning the implementation and adoption of Scrum.

- Coaching stakeholders in the use of the Scrum framework.

- Helping them understand their roles and encouraging buy-in.

- Influencing for changes in the organization – such as tackling ineffective constraints – that increase the team's productivity.

Chapter Nine deals with organization coaching in more depth.

In our pizza takeaway business, Dante's, the owner's son Joe will be acting as the Scrum Master. He has worked in software development for a while, and has been a project manager.

Behavior patterns for Scrum Masters

In order to support the Delivery Team and Product Owner, the Scrum Master should typically exhibit the following behaviors:

- Be honest about the team's performance.

- Use the Sprint Retrospective to help the team to improve.

- Know Scrum, the agile manifesto and its underlying principles well enough to explain them quickly and in detail.

- Have the final say on the correct way to follow Scrum.

- Enforce time constraints for all time-boxed activities, e.g. the Daily Scrum should last no longer than 15 minutes.

- Communicate directly with the team's stakeholders.

- Shield the team from interruptions.

- Make time to respond promptly to the team's questions.

- Facilitate the team in establishing their working agreement, definition of ready, and definition of done.

- Organize training and provide coaching as required to support continual improvement.

- Never tell the team how to solve a technical problem.

The team is also commonly called the *Development Team* and its members *Developers*. However, to avoid confusion with the role of programmer, this book uses *Delivery Team* and *team member*.

The team size should be six plus or minus three (i.e. from three to nine people) excluding the Product Owner and Scrum Master.

The Delivery Team

The Delivery Team needs to be empowered to self-organize, to determine the best solution for each feature, and to optimize their approach for both efficiency and effectiveness. This requires a certain combination of characteristics, skills, and behaviors.

Characteristics of the Delivery Team

The team should ideally have the following characteristics:

- Self-contained and cross-functional, possessing all the skills and knowledge necessary for delivery of the product.

- Self-organizing: no-one (including the Product Owner and Scrum Master) tells them how to do their work.

- While the team will program, test, and document, there are no discipline-based titles – everyone is a team member.

- Overall accountability for delivery of Product Increments belongs collectively to the whole team.

- They are not divided into sub-teams that separately focus on areas such as programming, testing, or documentation.

Team size

The team should be small enough to stay flexible, and large enough to get the work done. The ideal size of a team is between five and nine people (without counting the Product Owner and Scrum Master). While teams can be effective with as few as three members, with fewer than five they risk lacking some of the core skills necessary to release a Product Increment. With more than nine, the communications overhead makes the team too complex.

Having the right specialist skills in the team

For a team to produce high-quality functional Product Increments each and every Sprint, the team needs to include people who are very good at each of the following skill sets:

- User experience thinking, and business or process analysis.

- Proficiency in technical skills, such as programming.

- Expertise in testing tools, both manual and automated.

- Deploying software into different environments for integration, verification, and launch.

Our pizza takeaway, Dante's, has brought together a team of eight: five developers, two testers, and an analyst who can also do user-experience design and write web copy.

The importance of generalist as well as specialist skills
For the team to be high-performing, they need to be capable of covering for one another. Build the team around people who combine deep technical knowledge in one discipline, with a broad understanding of other disciplines. This encourages them to see events from each other's perspective and to fill in for each other.

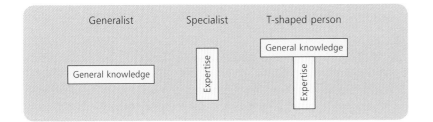

This combination of deep knowledge with broad understanding has led some to refer this model as representing **T-shaped** people.

Behavior patterns for team members
In order to work effectively and productively, Delivery Team members should typically share the following behavioral patterns:

- Work with only one team and one Sprint Backlog.

- Be a full-time member of the team, minimizing other duties.

- Actively seek to help fellow team members.

- Commit to doing whatever it takes to reach the Sprint goal.

- Accept coaching and feedback from team members and the Scrum Master, and be willing to learn any new skills needed.

- Pull a new Task from the Sprint Backlog as soon as an earlier Task has been completed, and in priority order.

- Share known impediments and risks as soon as possible.

- Attend every Scrum event in person.

- Never direct or manage the work of any other team member.

Even when team members might also be technical leads, any people for whom they have responsibility should not be in the same team.

Working well together

You should not expect that you can throw a group of people together and achieve high performance from the outset. It takes time and special conditions to make an effective team.

Collaboration is key

People work together in one of three operating modes; individualist, cooperative or collaborative:

- **Individualist** involves poor communication, failing to deal with issues, and often working against each other.

- **Cooperative** involves sharing responsibilities and communicating effectively, so they start to meet expectations.

- **Collaborative** involves building on each other's strengths and knowledge, to create something beyond the individual.

To be collaborative requires negotiation, challenging assumptions, and learning from each other. A simple example could be: programmers and testers collaborating to determine what and how to test, reducing testing effort and discovering problems earlier.

Collaboration is valued so highly that people just cooperating or working as individuals are called a group rather than a team.

How Scrum helps with collaboration

Scrum requires people to work together in a cross-functional manner, breaking down barriers between disciplines, and being accountable together for what the whole team produces.

By setting a Scrum Team up to be self-organizing, and authorizing it to find the most appropriate way to solve their problems, the team becomes empowered to break down those barriers.

Scrum practices such as Sprint Planning and the Daily Scrum encourage a team to collaborate and build relationships. Sprint Planning enables them to decide in advance how they might collaborate, whereas the Daily Scrum encourages them to identify opportunities to collaborate in the moment to maintain progress.

The Sprint Review gives a sense of accomplishment to the team's work, helping motivate and reinforce the value of collaboration.

Finally, the Sprint Retrospective allows them to consider how they work together and provide feedback on how they might improve.

Colocating the team

The best way for a team to collaborate on their Sprint goal is to be **colocated** – in the same physical space – for the whole Sprint, with the Product Owner and Scrum Master as much as possible.

Advantages of working in the same space

Whenever people work together in the same space, productivity and morale increase significantly, in three fundamental ways:

- **Feedback is immediate**: anyone on the team can see or hear what is going on and can speak up immediately if required – the team makes more progress, rather than being delayed by overnight emails, video conferences, or missed chat messages.

- **Conversation gains context**: rather than suffering death by email, people collaborate – the team Swarms (organizes) around priority Product Backlog Items and gets them quickly completed – any questions are promptly answered.

- **Being face-to-face makes a difference**: a large proportion of our communication is non-verbal, such as facial expressions and body language – standing together with a whiteboard can resolve misunderstandings immediately.

The space put aside at Dante's has 10 small desks, enough for the Delivery Team, the Product Owner, and the Scrum Master.

Coping with distributed teams

It is not always possible for the whole Scrum Team to be colocated. They may be distributed due to being based in different offices, outsourcing, off-shoring, or even working from home.

Distributed teams need appropriate collaboration and communication tools: such as video-conferencing, shared screens, instant messaging, and a digital agile management tool.

Everyone should still attend key events, like the Daily Scrum. This means negotiating a time that works across time zones, such as late afternoon in the US and early morning for New Zealand.

Where possible, distributed teams should try to meet in person for a kick-off session, such as Release Planning. This helps build relationships so they know they are dealing with real people. It also helps to rotate team members at other sites for a while. This fosters cultural connectedness and more open communication.

As a relatively new term, there are acceptable alternate spellings: colocation, co-location, and collocation.

Working agreements

A **working agreement** is a set of ground rules that a self-organizing team uses to establish behavioral norms without having them imposed by the organization or by a manager. It is established and changed only by mutual consent, by and with the whole team. This is also often known as a *social contract*.

Having a working agreement helps to define how the team want to work together and to make this transparent to the organization. Team members can more easily hold each other to account for their behavior and agree with the rest of the organization an acceptable way to interact. An example from Dante's below:

Dante's Working Agreement

- We must have a clear Sprint Goal and stay focused on it
- We will not accept Product Backlog items that are not ready
- We will never accept new items into the Sprint once it has started
- We always ensure we are ready for Sprint Review the night before
- We prioritize defects and bugs as soon as they are found
- We share risks and impediments as soon as they are found

- Our core hours are 10am to 4pm
- We will be on time for all Scrum events, or bring cookies next time
- We communicate – face-to-face is best, then Messenger, then email
- We all have a voice – use the talking stick to ensure we all listen
- Do not disturb – when the flag is up or headphones are on
- We respect personal space – do not talk across another person
- We respect team space – take care not to disturb other teams

Beware

Managers should not draw up the working agreement for a team. Instead, the team should be encouraged to establish their own.

Creating and adapting a working agreement

A working agreement reflects a team's context and experience, which makes it unique to each team. While the initial working agreement will be established during team formation, individual ground rules may be added or changed after Sprint Retrospectives. For example, should an impediment persist or recur over several Sprints, the team should consider whether they need to add a new behavior to their working agreement.

How to use a working agreement

As the working agreement is created and collectively owned by the whole team, it is each member's responsibility to follow the ground rules and manage their own behavior. To assist the team with keeping to their agreed behaviors, the working agreement should be displayed prominently, often next to the Scrum Board.

A note on non-Scrum roles

Except for a team working in a new start-up or a completely *greenfield* new product, most teams will be working with a number of roles external to them.

While such roles are not defined by Scrum, they are nonetheless vital for the success of the Scrum Team.

Customers and stakeholders
Without customers and stakeholders we have no idea what to build. Teams who have direct access to their customers and stakeholders are far more successful in delivering value, as they will understand better why certain functionality is required.

Shared services for specialist roles
Although teams are expected to be cross-functional and multi-disciplined, there are often specialized skills which may be required on an occasional basis only. For example, database administration or business intelligence. Many organizations choose to group specialized disciplines into a system team that supports several Scrum Teams (see Chapter Ten for more on this).

Business Analysts
Teams should include people who are capable of business analysis, such as documenting scenarios or mapping out processes. However, many organizations still have a specific role for a business analyst.

They may be part of a Delivery Team, hold a dual role as Product Owner and Business Analyst, work as part of a shared services team, or fulfill more of a change management role.

Project Managers
While there is no formal project management responsibility in Scrum, product development is often still organized and funded through projects. Where this is the case, the Project Manager focuses less on managing the Project Team and more on managing dependencies and integration with the rest of the organization.

Line Managers
Finally, while Scrum Teams are intended to be self-organizing, there is still a role for line management. Someone still needs to facilitate professional development opportunities, review performance, award pay increases, and approve holiday requests.

Summary

- The heart of the Scrum framework is the Scrum Team, consisting of three core roles: a Product Owner, Delivery Team, and Scrum Master.

- The Product Owner is responsible for the business value of the product, defining why and selecting what gets done.

- The Scrum Master ensures that the team is motivated, productive, and applying their agreed principles and practices.

- The Delivery Team is a self-organizing team of programmers, testers, and analysts – responsible for deciding how the work gets done and completing it.

- The team should have all the skills and experience necessary to be able to analyze, build, test, and deploy the product.

- Team members should have enough general knowledge of each others' specialist areas to be able to support one another.

- The team should have between five and nine team members; while three may be sufficient, this seldom allows enough capacity to be flexible.

- The behavior of the whole Scrum Team should be aligned with Scrum's values of focus, courage, openness, commitment, and respect.

- The team should focus on being collaborative rather than just cooperating or working as individuals.

- The whole Scrum Team should work together in the same physical space, if at all possible.

- Where teams are not able to be together all the time, they must have access to the same information in a timely manner, and have the tools to collaborate virtually.

- The team should capture their working agreement in a social contract, reference it whenever they have concerns about behavior, and update it after the Sprint Retrospective if some problems persist.

- The team need to understand roles outside their team and how they should best work with them.

3 Discovering what customers need

Before the team can deliver a product, the Product Owner has to define what it is they should build. This chapter explores how to define the Product Vision and high-level deliverables.

Hot tip

The Stanford D.School and British Design Council have each made significant contributions to *Design Thinking*.

Design thinking in Discovery

Many people start with a solution already in mind. This is not likely to meet what customers need. All too often we second-guess the customer or make assumptions based on what we have always done. There is, however, a track record of organizations achieving success by being mindful of customers' needs and exploring options before committing.

This is known as **Design Thinking** and has been summarized in a framework known as the *Double Diamond design process*. We switch thinking modes, between exploration – to generate options – and selection – to focus in on the best option. This is reflected in how the lines expand and contract, forming a diamond shape:

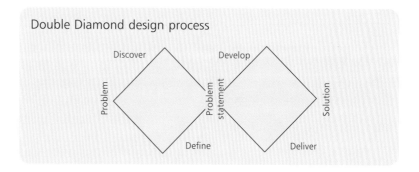

Double Diamond design process

Discover and Define
From the initial idea or inspiration for a new product, you can broaden your perspective in an attempt to discover a range of Delivery options. These Delivery options are assessed to confirm which are viable, feasible, and desirable. At this point, some may be combined with others, held back, or even rejected.

These selected Delivery options must then be defined sufficiently so that the Delivery Team can consider what might be involved in developing them. At this point, Delivery options are still quite broad, covering all the features necessary to help a customer achieve a specific goal.

Develop and Deliver
During Delivery, the team breaks these options down, on a just-in-time basis, into smaller slices of work that can be delivered within a single Sprint. By following this approach, the team is able to iteratively and incrementally build the product over an agreed number of Sprints.

The challenges with delivering early and often

As a feedback-driven framework for product development, Scrum recommends releasing completed work to customers as early and as often as possible. The ideal is to release work immediately after it has been approved as Done. However, many organizations do not have the capability to release completed work continuously in this way.

Alternatively, in Scrum, a team could deliver what they have completed at the end of each Sprint. This can also challenge larger organizations that might have an involved Release process and a legacy of existing systems with which they have to integrate.

For this reason, many Product Owners choose to release work after several Sprints. It is fairly common for larger organizations to release once per quarter, after six Sprints or so. This is better than releasing just once per year, or even less frequently, as is common in many organizations who are not yet following an agile approach like Scrum. However, it is always better to evolve your capability toward releasing work in smaller batches more often.

In the remainder of this chapter we explore how to carry out each of the following steps:

Beware

Releasing work infrequently, in large batches, is not the best way to get feedback from customers.

33

1. Build a Discovery Team and ensure that all the relevant stakeholders are involved

2. Run a series of Discovery workshops in order to define what product features are to be included

3. Develop the Product Vision to be clear about what exactly the Product Owner is going to take to market

4. Make the Product Vision real by using tools such as a Vision Statement, Value Proposition Canvas, or Vision Box

5. Include the customer's perspective, by identifying the primary customers and creating personas for them

6. Identify the capabilities required of the product in order to have impact on the customer

Building the Discovery Team

Before rushing to start development, the Product Owner first needs to ensure they understand their customers – what goals they are looking to achieve – then assess whether this could lead to a product they can operate successfully.

This means they need to include the customer as well as business and technical stakeholders. The first step towards this is establishing a **Discovery Team**. In some organizations, this might be called a Program Team or Core Product Team, who take on responsibility for overseeing the whole release cycle.

Who to include in the Discovery Team

The Product Owner needs to balance input from a range of stakeholders and perspectives all the way through development:

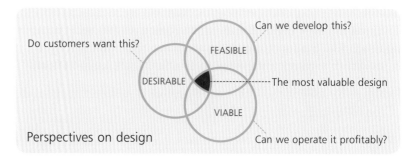

Perspectives on design

1. The voice of the customer: the Product Owner needs a perspective of the market to deliver a product that is **desirable** to customers and prospects

2. The needs of the enterprise: the Product Owner should involve operational stakeholders, such as sales and support, to ensure the product is **viable**

3. The Product Owner should involve technical stakeholders, such as architects, to ensure the product is **feasible**

4. For complex products, they should engage representatives from services on which they are dependent

5. On new products it may also be useful to involve those who can contribute with market research or prototyping

Hot tip

Some organizations involve the whole Delivery Team during product discovery, but most use only key representatives plus specific capabilities from outside the team.

Discovery workshops

Once the Product Owner has established their Discovery Team, they will need to allow sufficient time with them to establish who is the customer, their problems and needs, and potential solutions.

This will typically be through a series of facilitated workshops. While these are not formally a part of the Scrum framework, they will lead to greater confidence in the chosen product design.

These workshops help frame the opportunity, identify and empathize with the customer, focus on specific needs, generate ideas, then assess and define those ideas ready for Delivery.

You could class these up-front workshops as a **Design Sprint**, to differentiate it from Sprints that deliver Product Increments. A Delivery Team that has already been formed will also typically be preparing their environment ready for starting their first Sprint. For this reason, an alternative naming convention for this time is **Sprint 0**.

Outputs of Discovery workshops

The goal of these workshops is to help the Product Owner to define their product sufficiently so that a competent Delivery Team can deliver valuable Product Increments from the very first Sprint.

To set up the Delivery Team for success, the Product Owner will work with the Discovery Team to:

- Create a Product Vision.

- Produce an initial high-level breakdown of the work.

- Assess its complexity and value.

- Identify any potential Risks and agree on steps that might help reduce risk and complexity.

Discovery and Delivery in parallel

While Discovery workshops are followed by Delivery Sprints, this should not be considered a linear approach. Discovery cannot stop once Delivery has started. Just as Delivery is iterative and incremental, good Product Owners will continue to run Discovery workshops in parallel with Product Delivery, helping ensure that new Features are assessed and defined as they are identified.

The Product Vision

The first step for any Product Owner is to be clear about what they are intending to take to market.

True North

It is unfortunately all too common that Scrum Teams just get started working on the highest priority work without really understanding the customer, their needs, or why your organization might want to provide something to meet those needs.

Visualize the development as a journey. If the team doesn't know their eventual destination it is easy to get lost, and when the inevitable wrong-turn gets taken, it is harder to get back on track. They need a compass bearing or their **True North**.

From this perspective, the minimum deemed necessary for a Scrum Team to start should be a Product Vision and a Product Backlog. These cover *why* the product is being developed as well as *what* it needs to do.

A compelling purpose

Having a clear Product Vision paints a compelling picture that helps people see the future the Product Owner is envisioning. It defines the customer, their problems or opportunities, and the experience and benefits they envisage for the customer.

This helps to create a sense of purpose around a value proposition for the customer. As such, it should ideally be aspirational, while still being feasible to build and viable to operate.

Qualities of a Product Vision

As with any important goal, a well-crafted Product Vision needs to appeal as much to the emotions as to the intellect.

The vision should provide clarity for the future state of the product, while at the same time allowing sufficient leeway to adapt to feedback as it is developed and released incrementally.

It should also be easy enough to be recalled without reference and short enough to be explained in the time it takes to travel in an elevator. For this reason it is sometimes also referred to as the Elevator Pitch.

The following pages cover a range of techniques for helping define Product Vision.

Developing a Product Vision

There are a number of techniques for developing a Product Vision. Each helps to describe the potential market, a problem or opportunity to be solved, and the unique selling points. The following have all been shown to work with Scrum Teams.

The Metaphor or Screenwriter's Pitch

The easiest way to pitch a product is to use a powerful metaphor. This describes the product using recognizable terms, which makes it easy to relate to and more easily recalled.

To create a good metaphor for a product, it should be likened to another product or service from an alternate field. For example, the film Alien was first pitched as "*like Jaws in space*" and the video-sharing social media service Vimeo was described as "*like Flickr for movies*".

The Vision Statement/Elevator Pitch

To make the Product Vision slightly more descriptive, create a brief statement describing how the product helps the customer achieve their goal. To ensure that it contains all these attributes, you could follow a template similar to that below:

For [target customer]
who [has an identified need or dissatisfaction]
the [product name]
is a [category, type of thing]
that [key benefit, compelling reason to buy,
    what it enables the customer to do].
Unlike [alternative way of meeting the need],
our product [how it's better for the customer].

For a night-working IT developer
who is hungry but cannot go out for food
the Dante's pizza app
is a mobile ordering service
that lets you see all our menus, specials, and
    sides in your hand at any time.
Unlike a pizzeria, who you need to phone,
our app allows you to order from anywhere.

Making the vision real

Most organizations find visual techniques more compelling in communicating the full breadth of their vision.

Product Vision Board

The **Product Vision Board** has columns for target groups and their needs, with product benefits and how it could generate value.

Vision	What is your vision, your over-arching goal for building a new product?		
Target customer	**Needs**	**Product**	**Value**
Which market does the product address? Who are the target customers?	What problem does the product solve? How will it make the customer feel?	What is the product? What makes it desirable and special? Is it feasible to build?	How will the product benefit the company? Will it reduce costs, increase revenue, enter new market, etc.

This is often drawn up on a whiteboard or flip-chart, for the Discovery Team to brainstorm ideas with sticky-notes. Once they have been through the Discover and Define steps, the surviving sticky-notes could then be considered as delivery options.

Value Proposition Canvas

The **Value Proposition Canvas** provides more information on the target customer and product. Potential customers are explored to understand their goals (or jobs to be done), their current pain points, and their desired outcomes. The product is further defined to capture attributes that will relieve current pain or enable benefits. This helps to identify the degree of product fit.

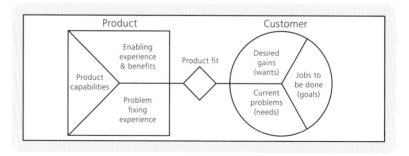

As with the previous example, this is typically drawn up in Discovery workshops and used to brainstorm with sticky-notes.

Product Vision Box

The last of these visual techniques also benefits from adding a tactile quality. The concept of the Vision Box is to visualize the product as if it were a packaged consumer product, such as soap powder or cereal.

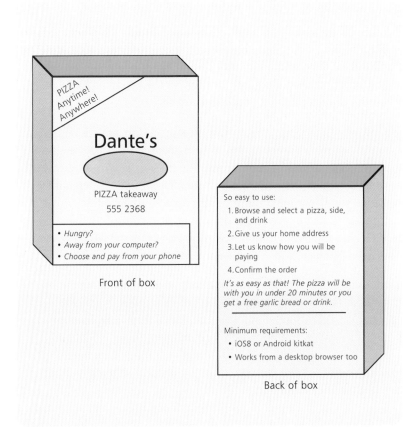

The front of the box should have the product name, an illustration, a snappy Vision Statement, and three key selling points. The back of the box should describe the high-level capabilities and the operating requirements.

While Discovery Teams can simulate the front and back of the box on A1 sheets, this is a more effective technique when made as a physical box. The Product Owner prepares a blank box, by pasting plain paper over an empty cereal or soap powder packet (for example), and then leads the team through the exercise.

The customer's perspective

A significant step in developing a clear Product Vision is to identify who are the most important customers (or prospects). Some advice on this suggests starting with a product feature and inventing a character that represents those who would most likely use that feature. This, however, can be too restrictive, as it limits thinking to what is currently possible rather than seeking to uncover unstated needs about the desired experience.

A compelling idea for a new or improved product is likely to have started from uncovering a real problem or opportunity. This means the Product Owner already had certain types of people in mind. Focus on them, and elaborate further on the likely types of people who will experience that problem in different ways.

Think about customers rather than market segments

Most products will serve a range of customers, and they will not all be carbon copies of each other. For this reason, organizations tend to segment their market to better target and understand it. However, these have traditionally been segmented by broad categories like age, gender, and income (for example). These don't tell a rich enough picture as they do not highlight why a customer might be interested in a particular product.

There will be factors that are unique to a problem space that serve better for segmentation. For example, a financial services organization might focus on attitude to risk, level of financial literacy, and approach to managing finances. This is a more human-centered approach and will result in a better understanding of the context, motivation, and perspective that drives customer behavior.

Bring customers to life with personas

As a feedback-driven product development framework, Scrum has to maintain a sharp focus on customers throughout Delivery as well as Discovery. Once the market segments have been clearly defined in human-centered terms, they should be translated into a form that is more easily referenced – that is, **Personas**.

Personas are an effective story-telling technique to bring abstract market segments to life, allowing you to walk in the shoes of your potential customers.

Beware

When thinking about how a system would be used, it is limiting to start from existing system capabilities as this often fails to uncover new needs.

Creating a customer persona

All personas for a product should be based on the same template. Some organizations choose to create well-designed personas that use photographs and are typeset and laminated to last longer. However, most organizations will keep them in hand-drawn and hand-written form, stuck on the wall.

Profile	Goals	
What behaviors does this persona represent?	Why would they use this product?	
Consider age, gender, job, experience, training, etc.	Their key job to be done, pain points, benefits being sought.	Persona Name

Name

Choose a name that describes the segment, e.g. "New Student Pizza Lover" or "Repeat Family Feast Customer". To make it feel more real, give the persona a real name. Alliteration helps people remember, so consider a surname based on the segment and a first name starting with the same sound. For example, "Steve Student" or "Fiona Feast". Alternatively, keep with the alliteration but use a more normal surname, such as "Steve Stone" or "Fiona Foster".

Profile

Create a brief character description, based on the characteristics and patterns that helped identify the market segment. Examples of areas to include are: their role, their experience, and their depth of knowledge.

Goals

When considering their motivation, it is important to factor in what they are looking to achieve – their *job to be done*. For example, one pizza customer may have friends round while another may be working late. Knowing why they might want the product helps to better align the product to their needs.

Mug shot

Lastly, create an image that brings this persona to life. It need only be a rough sketch of a head and shoulders, perhaps with an item that illustrates their problem or job to be done. For example, a laptop in one hand and a slice of pizza in the other.

Identifying deliverables

With a Product Vision defined and market segments illustrated as personas, the Product Owner next facilitates the Discovery Team in identifying the capabilities needed in their product. These will range from organizational – such as new skills and processes – to the technical – such as new software and infrastructure. As the capabilities are uncovered, this establishes a scope for work.

Mapping impact and deliverables

Impact Mapping is an effective technique for identifying these capabilities. An Impact Map is a mind-map created with the Discovery Team to visualize scope and uncover assumptions.

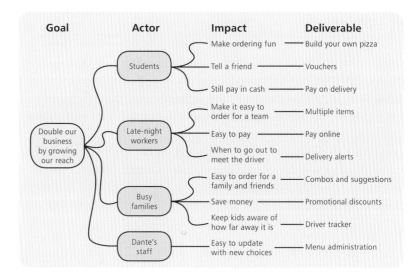

Business Goal

At the heart of the Impact Map is the goal. The Product Owner should start with a short form of the Product Vision for this.

Actor

The first level out defines who will help or hinder us in achieving the Product Vision. The obvious first candidates for this level are the customer personas identified earlier. These, however, are just the primary actors. The Product Owner should also consider secondary actors, those roles who assist in providing the service, such as customer service agents, or those who could block success, such as competitors. Like the customer personas, these secondary actors should also be named smartly, typically with a qualified role rather than a full persona name.

Impact

The next level identifies what impact each actor could have on the product; the behavior that could be expected if they were to help or hinder us in achieving the goal.

If the Discovery Team has already developed customer personas, there will already be a list of jobs to do. When your customers can fulfill their own goals with this product, that will help you achieve yours. This ensures that Product Discovery stays focused on the customer rather than just generating a list of all the Features imaginable.

When done comprehensively, this will likely generate many more impacts than are strictly necessary for you to create a compelling product. There may also be impacts that either duplicate or conflict with others. The full set of impacts should be thought of as options, and the scope for Delivery drawn around those that are more likely to help you achieve your goal.

Deliverable

The lowest level defines the capabilities that you require to enable the actors to achieve the impacts identified, or to mitigate any negative impact that detractors might have.

Although the lowest level on the Impact Map, the deliverables will still be at a high level. They are not yet defined as Product Backlog Items. As described for impacts above, there will often be far more deliverables than you can likely afford. However, they will help in determining the scope and will act as a seed for identifying the Features.

Tracing everything back to the goal

By identifying and grouping deliverables in this way, everything can be traced back to the Product Vision and goal. It makes it easier to identify potential work that would not add value, before it is even defined, sized, and prioritized.

Each link in the chain from goal to actor, from actor to impact, and from impact to deliverable represents an assumption. By capturing these in the Impact Map in such a visual way, it also makes it far easier to discuss such assumptions with key stakeholders.

Summary

- Before a Delivery Team can be involved in developing a product, the Product Owner first has to ensure that they have a clear vision, a breakdown of the work, and an assessment of any potential risks and dependencies.

- The Product Owner should establish a Discovery Team that represents the customer as well as the operational and technical sides of the organization.

- For products which are heavily integrated with services from other organizations, it would be useful to involve representatives from them too.

- Discovery workshops allow the Product Owner to work with the Discovery Team to explore what customers want and what features they need in a product.

- Discovery workshops adopt techniques from design thinking, to search out a number of possible options before committing to a solution.

- Discovery is not just up front, in Scrum there is a parallel cycle of Discovery alongside Delivery too.

- The Product Owner needs to create a clear Product Vision – this provides ongoing guidance to both the Discovery Team and the Delivery Team.

- There are many techniques a Product Owner can use to craft the Product Vision, including: the Metaphor, the Elevator Pitch, the Vision Board, the Proposition Canvas, and the Product Vision Box.

- The voice of the customer is often represented through the proxy of personas – these lay out key attributes of each major type of customer, along with what goals or problems they have which the product could address.

- Impact mapping is a useful technique for exploring all potential stakeholders, what impact they could have on the success of the product, and what capabilities are required in the product to help stakeholders achieve those impacts.

4 Defining the Product Backlog

The Product Backlog contains all the work the team needs to complete in order to deliver the Product. This chapter covers how to define the product, ensuring everything is captured early enough to reduce risk, and late enough to maximize flexibility.

The Product Backlog

The **Product Backlog** is the prioritized requirements list for all new Features, enhancements, and fixes to the product.

As the Product Backlog should be the only source of work for the team, everything needed for the product must be on it. However, it is not expected that it be fully discovered and defined up front.

The Product Backlog is dynamic and evolving. It starts out as a high-level list of required capabilities and becomes more detailed as the product is built, feedback is obtained, and people identify what is needed to be competitive, appropriate, and useful.

Product Backlog Items

The work the team needs to do includes Feature development, Bug fixing, and team improvements. These are called Product Backlog Items (PBIs) and are described on the pages that follow.

Each PBI must have a title, a description, an indication of potential value and how that will be validated, the likely size of the work, and any associated risks and dependencies.

The order of items on the Product Backlog indicates the order in which they will be done. The closer a PBI is to the top of the list, the more important it is that it be implemented soon. The closer a PBI is to being worked on, the more detailed it has to be – so items at the top of the Product Backlog are more detailed and narrow in scope (such as Stories), while those at the bottom are more abstract and broad (such as Epics).

A Bug is something unwanted that stops the product performing as it should (see page 114).

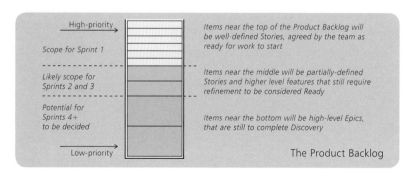

High-priority

Scope for Sprint 1

Likely scope for Sprints 2 and 3

Potential for Sprints 4+ to be decided

Low-priority

Items near the top of the Product Backlog will be well-defined Stories, agreed by the team as ready for work to start

Items near the middle will be partially-defined Stories and higher level features that still require refinement to be considered Ready

Items near the bottom will be high-level Epics, that are still to complete Discovery

The Product Backlog

Definition of Ready

In order for PBIs to be brought into Sprint Planning, the team has to be satisfied that they are Ready, having previously agreed the definition of what Ready means.

Backlog Refinement

Backlog Refinement is the ongoing process where the Product Owner and the Delivery Team collaborate on getting the PBIs ready, adding detail, updating assessments, and re-prioritizing.

Continued evolution

When customers can actively use the product and provide feedback, this will add to the Product Backlog. As business needs or market conditions change, the Product Backlog will continue to evolve, as long as the product is in use.

Rules of Scrum for the Product Backlog

- All items on the Product Backlog must relate to a single product (or system).

- The Product Backlog must be easily visible to all stakeholders (e.g. as cards on a wall or in a digital agile management tool).

- Any stakeholder (e.g. team member, salesperson, or even a customer) can suggest a new PBI.

- The Product Owner owns the responsibility for the order in which PBIs are prioritized, although it is good practice that they involve others in the process.

- The Scrum Team collaborates on refining the Product Backlog to ensure it is ready for Sprint Planning.

- PBIs are ordered so that no two PBIs have the same priority in the Product Backlog.

- Known Bugs and Defects generally should be ordered at the top of the Product Backlog to be worked on next.

- The top PBIs (of whatever type) should be small enough that several can fit into a single Sprint.

- PBIs should be *vertical slices* through the solution that achieve something of value (e.g. not just a screen, but the ability to update a database and return a response).

- PBIs should have enough detail for an informed conversation, rather than containing full specifications up front.

Product Backlog Items

As an ordered list of everything that the team might need to do, Product Backlog Items (PBIs) cover a broad range of work:

- Epics, Features, and Stories define the functionality we want, from high-level capabilities to detailed workings of features.

- Bugs, Defects, and Incidents capture anything we don't want in the product (see page 114).

- Spikes enable the team to reduce risk by investigating anything they are unsure of (see page 94).

- Team improvements allow the time to invest in becoming a more effective team (see page 147).

All PBIs for one product must be in a single Product Backlog. This makes it easier to value and size them together, and the team is not distracted by working with more than one Product Owner.

Stories

A **Story** describes a discrete part of the overall product's functionality. These act as the building blocks for the product.

Historically, Stories were hand-written on index cards. Today, they are typically created and tracked in a digital agile management tool. Most tools allow Stories to be printed, so that the team can track them on a physical Scrum Board if they choose.

The Story describes functionality that enables a customer to achieve a specific job. This should be kept brief and written in everyday business language, to prompt a conversation at the time of doing the work. This is typically in the format of a **User Story**:

Don't forget

The User Story was originally described as the 3Cs – standing for *Card, Conversation and Confirmation* – and originated with Extreme Programming (XP).

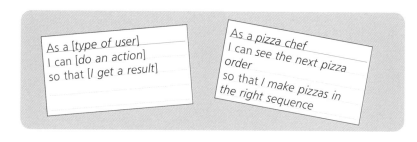

As a [type of user]
I can [do an action]
so that [I get a result]

As a pizza chef
I can see the next pizza order
so that I make pizzas in the right sequence

The User Story would be on the front of the index card, while the Acceptance Criteria (see page 51) would be written on the back. These describe how the Product Owner will approve the work.

Epics

An **Epic** typically describes an entire workflow, so is often written up as a Use Case which covers every interaction (see page 57).

As the highest level of functionality, Epics are large and broadly-defined. When it is time to plan the work into Sprints, they are broken down into smaller PBIs (i.e. Features or Stories).

Epics are often named with an action and an object; for example, "*Ordering from a smartphone*" or "*Setting up a new promotion*". However, for Product Owners who visualize their Product scope with an Impact Map (see Chapter Three), Epics are likely to be derived from the deliverables they identified. An Epic could then be described with a User Story:

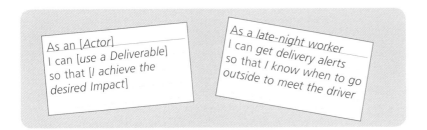

As an [Actor]
I can [use a Deliverable]
so that [I achieve the desired Impact]

As a late-night worker
I can get delivery alerts
so that I know when to go
outside to meet the driver

Features

Many Product Owners find that two levels of product decomposition is enough, and stick with just Epics and Stories. However, for products that are large and complex or that involve multiple teams, Product Owners will also use a **Feature** as a planning and decomposition level between an Epic and its Stories.

Comparative size of Epics, Features, and Stories

As a rough indication, a Story should be completed within a single Sprint, a Feature may take two or more Sprints, and while an Epic may take several Sprints, it must be completed within a Release.

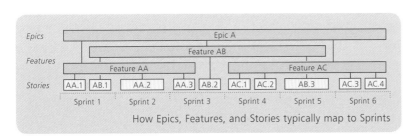

Epics	Epic A					
Features		Feature AB				
		Feature AA			Feature AC	
Stories	AA.1 AB.1	AA.2	AA.3 AB.2	AC.1 AC.2	AB.3	AC.3 AC.4
	Sprint 1	Sprint 2	Sprint 3	Sprint 4	Sprint 5	Sprint 6

How Epics, Features, and Stories typically map to Sprints

Don't forget

It is always better to finish work and get feedback, to learn what could be done better. Any extra large Epic PBIs should be split so that they can be completed within a single Release.

Invest in a well-formed Backlog

There is an art-form to crafting Product Backlog Items (PBIs) that are truly fit for purpose. They need to meet the multiple needs of communicating the intent of the Product Owner, be easy to understand for the team, and flexible enough to be used for ongoing discovery, planning, and delivery.

There is a widely accepted set of criteria or key attributes of what makes a PBI well-formed. When a PBI does not meet all of these criteria, the team may want it rewritten, re-scoped, broken down, or potentially even discarded completely.

These criteria form a checklist to assess the quality of a PBI, and are made more memorable through the acronym of INVEST:

- **Independent**: the Product Owner should be able to move PBIs around easily to change the order in which Product Features will be developed – so PBIs should be reasonably independent of each other.

- **Negotiable**: a PBI's description is necessarily brief, and requires conversation closer to the time of being developed – this allows the Product Owner to limit commitment to as late as responsible, e.g. to allow for changing requirements.

- **Valuable**: every PBI must have some discernible value, whether it is the functionality it provides the customer, the feedback and insight it will provide, or how it enables some other function – this is the "so that [I get a result]" clause in the User Story format.

- **Estimatable**: a PBI must be defined well enough that the team can assess how they might develop a solution for it, and be relatively certain of the complexity, risk, and effort involved.

- **Small**: at the Epic and Feature level, PBIs will be larger than can fit in a single Sprint – a Story should be sized such that a team could complete it with a few days of effort.

- **Testable**: it should be clear how the team will know when they have delivered what is required of a PBI – the Product Owner needs to provide unambiguous Acceptance Criteria (see page 51) and the team should be able to generate testable examples to prove or disprove these.

Beware

Any Story larger than a few days of effort will often have hidden risks or complexities that result in the team developing the wrong solution, taking too long, or failing to complete it.

Acceptance Criteria

A Story is a brief description of a goal or job to be done, that a customer should be able to achieve using a Feature of the product. **Acceptance Criteria** help build on this, defining how the Product Owner will confirm that the work is Done and ready for Release.

Acceptance Criteria are statements that define what the product must and must not do, that specify both functional requirements (e.g. how the functionality enables someone to achieve a goal) and non-functional requirements (e.g. access and authentication).

Each criterion should have a clear pass or fail condition; there can be no partial acceptance. They define the boundaries of the work and provide certainty to the team for when a Story can be considered complete and working as required.

Well-defined Acceptance Criteria

The language used must be clear, help programmers understand how their code will be tested, and help testers understand what they should test. They should be relatively simple in language, while still providing enough precision to be useful.

Acceptance Criteria must state the intent, not the solution. The phrasing should be the same, regardless of the platform the application is intended for – desktop, web, or smartphone.

For example, *"Can accept the pizza order into the queue"* rather than *"Can click the Accept button to add the pizza to the queue"*.

Types of Acceptance Criteria

Acceptance Criteria cover everything that is important to test that a Story is working as required. Typical examples include:

- **Functional**: defines the functions the Story will introduce – for example, *"Can list all available pizzas on the menu"*.

- **Non-functional**: defines the conditions the Story must meet – for example, *"Cannot confirm order if not logged on"*.

- **Performance**: where speed of response, availability, or scalability is critical to the acceptance of an individual Story, it should be explicitly included – for example, *"Response time must be under two seconds"*.

Specification by example

To mitigate the risk of making assumptions, when defining Acceptance Criteria the team should make conditions more concrete by defining examples for the more abstract requirements.

Making Acceptance Criteria specific with examples

For example, Karly, our Product Owner, has created a story to encourage potential shoppers with a discount on their first order.

The team initially assumed this would affect whole orders for new customers. However, when they explored examples, they found that a customer could choose to sign up but not order, and that if a product is on special offer it should not get additional discount.

How to specify the example

While the examples should be specific, they should also be written in plain language. For example, "*Discount applied to customer's first order only*" and "*Discounts not applied to products on special offer*".

In order for testers to convert such examples into test cases more easily, it helps when it is clearer what condition the product should be in already, what event triggers the functionality, and the expected results. The format for this is known as **Gherkin**:

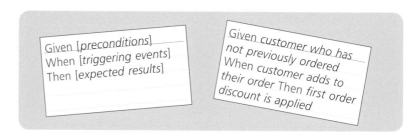

Given [preconditions]
When [triggering events]
Then [expected results]

Given customer who has not previously ordered When customer adds to their order Then first order discount is applied

To provide good test coverage, this should be repeated using examples that show items that are and are not on special offer, and customers who have and who have not previously ordered.

Future-proofing the product

Although created to confirm that one Story meets its Acceptance Criteria, key examples should be kept and reused to check whether any future changes affect the integrity of this functionality.

Defining examples for Acceptance Criteria in this way is a prerequisite for behavior-driven development (see Chapter Seven), and it helps significantly when it comes to automating tests.

Supplementing Acceptance Criteria with examples creates the most detailed level of specification on a Scrum development.

Keep these examples to use for regression testing in future Sprints.

Definition of Ready

In order for the Delivery Team to make best use of their time in a Sprint, it is critical that the Product Backlog has sufficient items that are ready for the team to consider in Sprint Planning. It must be clear what has to be done so that the team can identify the Tasks and be ready to start work immediately.

Where the Product Owner does not have anything Ready, the team cannot work on the next Product Increment. They lose vital development time by extending the planning event or undertaking Discovery and Refinement when they should have started work.

What constitutes Ready is rarely the same between organizations, or even between teams. It is good practice for the Product Owner to have agreed with the team what needs to be done in order for Product Backlog Items (PBIs) to be Ready. For example:

While a *Definition of Ready* helps a team be more confident in the work they are asked to do, there will always be times when the team is prepared to take on important work that is not fully Ready.

> ## Dante's Definition of Ready
>
> - *Must have name, description, and Acceptance Criteria with examples.*
> - *Must meet principles of INVEST.*
> - *Dependent work has been identified and completed / or someone has committed to it being done in time.*
> - *Must have been prioritized.*
> - *Any risks have been identified and mitigated (e.g. with a Spike).*
> - *No Story should be a surprise at Sprint Planning.*
> - *The team knows how to present or demonstrate this at the review.*
> - *The team is confident they can build, test, and deliver in 1 Sprint.*

A word of caution

It is easy for a team to use the Definition of Ready to force all the analysis and design work to be done outside of the Sprint. While this makes PBIs easier to assess and work on, it results in too much work up front before the PBI is confirmed and committed. It is therefore critical to strike the right balance of ensuring that the Definition of Ready is good enough to avoid ill-prepared work, while avoiding too much work being done ahead of time.

Keep it fresh

In the spirit of continual improvement, teams should be prepared to revise their Definition of Ready. If the team find that they are struggling with unprepared work, the Definition of Ready could be strengthened. If the Product Owner finds they are asked to do so much up front that work is delayed, it could be lightened.

Do not use the *Definition of Ready* like a stage-gate; this can make Scrum feel more like a plan-driven project.

The Discovery Board

As the team are working on the selected Stories each Sprint, it is still important that the team can see what might be coming up next. When they are refining the Product Backlog, they should be able to see what else might be involved later and advise the Product Owner of any potential risks and dependencies.

Just as Scrum Teams display their Delivery work in progress on a Scrum Board, many teams also like their Product Owner to display the Discovery work alongside on a separate **Discovery Board**. Ideally, the Impact Map would be adjacent to that too.

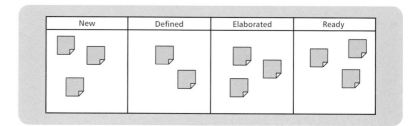

The Discovery Board represents the product Discovery process. While this means that the columns will be unique to each organization, they typically will cover prospective work that is new, defined, elaborated, and Ready:

- **New**: during Discovery workshops, the Discovery Team will consider whether recent feedback and insights should result in changes to the Impact Map, and then select the next most important deliverable(s).

- **Defined**: each deliverable typically will result in one or more Epic which need to be named and given a brief description – at this point, dependencies should start to be identified.

- **Elaborated**: as the likely Sprint to start work on an Epic draws near, the Discovery Team will start to break the Epic down into Features and Stories – for each of these they will agree Acceptance Criteria, assess any risk or dependency that might be mitigated through a Spike, and confirm when any dependent is likely to be completed.

- **Ready**: finally, when all dependent work has been done – including graphics, legal, web copy, etc. – the Stories would be agreed as candidates to be pulled into the next Sprint.

Backlog Refinement

To ensure that sufficient items on the Product Backlog meet the Delivery Team's Definition of Ready, the Product Owner and the Discovery Team need to keep working on the Product Backlog. This is done in a regular session called **Backlog Refinement**, which can be considered an extension of the Discovery workshops.

Refine in advance of Sprint Planning

Refining the Product Backlog runs in parallel with Delivery Sprints, and looks at upcoming work only, rather than at the work of the current Sprint.

The number of Sprints to prepare depends on several factors, including dependencies, the number of teams involved, and how complicated the technical environment is. Teams should allow enough time to reduce complexity and mitigate risk through Spikes (see Chapter Six), and for any dependent work to be completed.

- The recommendation is that teams refine their Product Backlog for two to three Sprints ahead.

- Refining any further ahead could mean detailing work that may become de-prioritized.

- On the other hand, refining less could mean the team does not have enough work ready for Sprint Planning.

While Backlog Refinement is not yet formally recognized as a Scrum event, the recommendation is to invest up to 10% of a team's time. Most Product Owners will schedule a weekly session for Backlog Refinement, typically of just one hour.

Refine for success

Ensuring that the Product Backlog is Ready makes Sprint Planning far more effective and efficient, because the Product Owner and team can start their planning with a clear, prioritized, and well-defined set of PBIs. It also helps the team stay clear about the potential upcoming work, as the Product Owner might have changed priorities since their Release Planning session.

Breaking down, defining, and agreeing what work might be required for the desired functionality also helps the Product Owner to make choices about what could be de-prioritized or removed altogether.

Backlog Refinement should never be used to carry out additional analysis on PBIs in the current Sprint Backlog.

Teams that do not refine their Product Backlog in advance, spend most of their Sprint Planning on questions, technical discussion, and confusion.

Add context with UX design

While Product Backlog Items (PBIs) are useful for capturing a discrete element of functionality required for a customer to achieve something of value, they are not so suited to describing overall interaction.

For Product Owners to communicate how a customer's goals will be met, they need a way to illustrate steps or activities over time, to design the User Experience (UX). This can take many forms, including workflows, customer journeys, Use Case Activity Diagrams, and Story Maps. Each has its own utility, and teams often use more than one together.

Workflows

A **workflow** is a simplified flowchart of the key activities that a customer needs to complete in order to achieve their outcome, normally illustrated as steps progressing from left to right. Each step should normally be named using an **[action]-[object]** pairing to describe what they are doing and what is affected.

Customer journeys

The workflow diagram can be made richer by illustrating it with the satisfaction level of each step in the workflow. Symbols or colors are often used to annotate the workflow steps, and sometimes the steps are positioned higher or lower, from good to poor, as the **customer journey** progresses left to right.

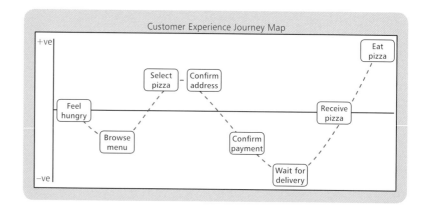

Hot tip

Workflows are useful as they can quickly be drawn on a whiteboard, and then photographed or captured easily in a diagramming tool.

Use Cases

A variant of the basic workflow, the **Activity Diagram** for **Use Cases** provides a summary of interactions between the customer and the product. A series of interactions are linked together into scenarios, with one main path – often called the *happy path* – and a series of alternate paths and exceptions. Each interaction will likely require one or more Stories to be implemented.

Use Cases are good for exploring and defining complete end-to-end interactions, including alternate paths and handling exceptions.

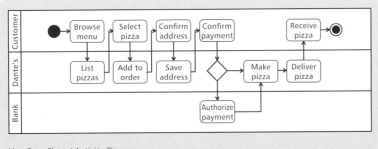

Use Case Flow / Activity Diagram

Story mapping

Story mapping uses a two-dimensional grid to show a sequence of activities and steps, moving left to right. This represents the end-to-end flow from the customer's perspective. Until detail is added, this is often referred to as a *walking skeleton*.

Under each step, the Story Map is then populated with Story PBIs that implement what's required for that step. These are ordered by priority, from top to bottom, with the option of identifying which should go together into a single Sprint or Release.

Story mapping helps make sense of a large Product Backlog and identifies potential gaps, and can be used in Discovery workshops.

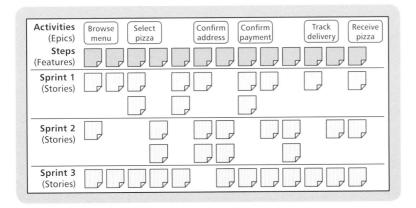

Patterns to discover work

While uncovering the capabilities needed by a product, it is critical to focus on the needs of the customer and how they will use it to achieve something of value to them. The format of the User Story encourages teams to identify with the customer and the actions they need to take – **As a <customer> I can <action>**.

However, this may only capture and define a subset of what the product needs to do. In order to create a product that is scalable, efficient, and effective, the team should consider what is needed from other perspectives.

For example, as well as the functionality needed to support customer interactions, they also need to consider all the channels to market, the data that needs to persist between sessions and transactions, and the Business Rules that ensure the functionality does what is intended. Finally, as the product is progressively defined, at all levels, they need to determine the qualifying constraints within which the product will be used, such as performance and security.

While this risks increasing the scope, many of the points uncovered will be implemented through better Acceptance Criteria on existing work as well as new work to be done.

Channels

In today's world, the channels through which customers can consume products and services is ever-growing. The Product Owner should spend time with customers and key internal stakeholders to identify all the potential channels.

Dante's might assume that they need to develop a smartphone app, but this might exclude some customers who cannot use this technology and would prefer a desktop-based web browser.

Data sources

Data is critical to any product or service. Understanding where data will be sourced and kept will flush out additional requirements. By identifying key collections of data, the Product Owner will be able to assess whether any additional functionality is required to create, update, and remove it.

Dante's might choose to integrate their stock management software so that a customer cannot order a pizza for which they do not have the ingredients.

Business Rules

Every product has to work within an organization's Business Rules, which are a set of constraints that define or limit what the organization is able to do. Such constraints may be imposed by regulation, by societal or market norms, by commercial necessity, or preference of the organization itself.

Dante's might allow a customer with an invalid credit card to come into the store and pay by cash, or they might offer additional discounts to customers who are willing to pick up their orders rather than have them delivered.

Dante's also need to ensure that they comply with the relevant commercial laws. Once they have accepted a payment for an order, they have formed a contract for delivery of that pizza.

Quality of service

In addition to the functional, technical, data, and business perspectives described above, you are likely to have overriding requirements that define the quality of service provided. These describe the conditions under which the product must remain effective or qualities that it must have, and include such concerns as availability, scalability, security, and performance.

Don't forget

Quality of service is also known as Non-Functional Requirements.

- **Availability**: the percentage of the time the business should be operational – Dante's want customers to be able to order online during their opening hours, so need to be 100% operational between the hours of 4 p.m. and midnight.

- **Scalability**: the maximum number of simultaneous transactions it should be capable of supporting – Dante's will have a limited roll-out initially, but if successful may wish to support ordering takeaways from their two restaurants as well.

- **Security**: controlling how open or protected each Feature is – while they want anyone to be able to browse and order, Dante's will restrict some Features for registered customers. They also need to take care with how they process credit card and other personally identifiable information.

- **Performance**: the time it takes for a response – for general usage, Dante's want average response times under 1.2 seconds. For ordering, they are willing to accept longer, especially for validating transactions with third-party credit card services.

The number and size of Stories a team can complete in a Sprint will vary – more experienced teams will tend to work on a higher number of smaller Stories, as this improves flow.

Patterns to break work down

When teams are successful in ensuring that their Product Backlog covers all the capabilities a product will require, it often ends up lumpy, with Stories that vary too much in size. Following the INVEST principles (see page 50), Stories should be small enough to be completed within a single Sprint.

Stories are often large because they are complex or have too many unknowns. By not breaking them down, the team risks not completing the work within a single Sprint. Breaking down larger Stories, or **Story Splitting**, helps by identifying a number of simpler Stories.

What size is the right size?

There is no single right size for Stories. This will vary between teams, and from Feature to Feature. However, an individual team should be able to assess what size is too large.

For example, in their fifth Sprint, the team at Dante's identified a repeating pattern that they seemed unable to complete 20-point Stories – so they agreed to limit themselves to 13 or under.

Teams can also calculate a nominal Story size. First, they should look at their **Velocity** (the average number of Story points they have delivered over the last few Sprints). A team of nine (made up of analysts, programmers, and testers) should be capable of completing around 6-10 Stories per Sprint. For most teams this means nothing larger than eight Story points.

During Backlog Refinement and Sprint Planning, this nominal size should trigger breaking down anything larger than that.

How to break down large work

There are many strategies to consider when breaking work down; 22 patterns have been included here, with examples.

Most Product Backlog Items (PBIs) could be broken down using any pattern, so it is important for a team to consider the purpose of each pattern and whether it seems appropriate for that PBI.

Some patterns uncover functionality that the Product Owner may be willing to prioritize for later Sprints, or even discard. Some patterns also help to reduce or remove Risks and Dependencies.

The aim is to derive Stories that are within the team's nominal size and that are not too small to break the principles of INVEST.

Any work split off should be added to the Product Backlog as separate items, to be considered in Backlog Refinement in their own right.

Workflow patterns

Large PBIs, like Epics, typically cover a whole end-to-end workflow, which – for all but the simplest product features – would be too much work for a single Sprint. By focusing on those steps the customer needs to reach their goal, these patterns help to break out smaller Stories that focus on parts of that.

- **Scenarios**: for complex workflows, there will often be a main path of interactions through the product that will be used the majority of the time – the main path will generate the greatest value, so should be developed before any lesser-used alternate paths.

   Dante's decided that ordering a pizza was the main path, while adding sides and drinks were alternate paths.

- **Beginning and end**: most workflows consist of a number of interactions over time, and while the full capability will require all the steps, the greatest value often comes from the beginning and the end – adding additional steps in between can come later.

   Dante's decided that ordering a pizza and collecting it from the store could be a complete workflow.

- **Single interaction**: a further straightforward approach to breaking a workflow down is to consider each individual interaction to be a separate story.

   Dante's created separate stories for viewing the menu, adding items to an order, viewing the order, removing items, and finally paying for it.

...cont'd

Complexity patterns

When a PBI already deals with a single interaction, but is still sized as too large to be completed in a single Sprint, the team should consider whether there are hidden complexities.

● **Acceptance Criteria and Business Rules**: where constraints have introduced complexity, make them clearer by specifying examples (see page 52), and then consider which may be independent and split these off into separate PBIs.

Dante's had one feature to handle ordering a pizza with a valid credit card, while the Acceptance Criteria for alternate scenarios – such as handling expired credit cards or pizzas they cannot make because they have run out of some ingredients – became Stories under a separate Feature.

● **Roles**: where the same functionality could be undertaken by more than one role, it is worth considering what the simplest role is that could be supported initially.

Dante's decided that enabling customers to place pizza orders themselves was more straightforward than having staff enter orders from telephone calls or walk-ins.

● **Conditions**: for PBIs that have a complicated set of conditions, consider grouping the conditions and breaking them out into separate PBIs.

When it came to applying discounts to the pizza order, Dante's chose to support discounts through a voucher code, and to later add automated capabilities, like handling the condition of a customer's first order.

● **Data variations**: where the same information could be stored and presented in different ways – such as the language used or how progress is reported – focus first on the most basic.

Dante's chose to launch in English and subsequently to support Spanish-speaking customers. They also chose to launch with simple messages that reflect the changing status of an order, and subsequently to illustrate progress as gradually filling in slices in a pizza pie chart.

Beware

Regulation may dictate that more than one *official* language has to be supported at launch.

- **Data operations**: each type of operation or action taken with data requires different functionality, so PBIs that deal with the generic administration of something will often include the need to be able to add new, list all or some, read details, update, and archive or delete – each of these can be considered a separate PBI.

  When Dante's want to manage their menu dynamically, they will need the ability to add new pizzas, update existing ones, and eventually to remove them from the menu.

- **User Interfaces**: sometimes there is complexity within the User Interface (UI) rather than the Business Rules or data – work could start with a simpler form of UI and then progressively enhance it in later Sprints.

  Dante's chose to display their menu initially as just text and photographs, then subsequently introduced the interactive ability to drag ingredients onto a "build your own" pizza base.

- **Channels**: for products that are likely to be delivered over a number of channels, the development for each could be handled separately.

  Dante's chose to start selling through a website, followed by an app for smartphones, and then one for tablets.

- **Cardinality**: complexity can arise from having to deal with more than one of something.

  Dante's chose to start with a single list of pizzas, then being able to page through pizzas, and finally to be able to switch between tabs of pizzas, starters, desserts, and drinks.

- **Data sources**: where the information to be displayed will be drawn from more than one source, it may be possible to focus first on the critical information from a single source, and then progressively add in the others.

  Dante's started with customers entering any text in as their address, then they chose to add capabilities for automatically validating it against a third-party database, and finally for detecting the address as the customers enter it and offer to auto-complete it for them.

Hot tip

Seeing the word *Manage* in a PBI title is a hint that it covers multiple operations and should be broken down.

...cont'd

Deferral patterns

While each PBI should be valuable, to meet the INVEST principles (see page 50) – that value can sometimes come from the feedback received from trying something out. Some value can also be derived from launching a simpler service and then enhancing it later, so it is worth considering whether there are any aspects of the work that can be split off and deferred to a later Sprint.

- **Manual to automated**: if a customer's goal can be reached with some steps being manual, then consider separating out the work to make those steps part of the software solution.

  Dante's could have started by collecting payment on delivery, and later added taking credit cards with the order.

- **Static to dynamic**: it may be possible to create a solution with some elements static, then load them dynamically, and finally make them searchable.

  Dante's hard-coded the pizza menu on the web-page, then subsequently had it loading from a database.

- **Transient to permanent**: while a product might eventually need to store information permanently, security concerns can make this costly, so consider not retaining customers' details.

  Dante's started with processing one-off card payments, then later saved details for faster future payments.

- **Exception handling**: while it is important that customers are provided with useful feedback if anything goes wrong during transactions, this does not have to be too complicated initially.

  Dante's started by giving customers a simple error message, then they logged exceptions to track with metrics, and finally considered allowing customers to submit an incident report.

- **Quality of service**: while a product may be destined for a mass market, it need not initially be built to be fully scalable and cope with performance at peak times.

  Dante's only needed to support one pizza takeaway store, later wanting to have the option of scaling up to support takeaway orders from their two other restaurants.

Beware

Take care when deferring quality of service, especially when a product or system already has a large customer base.

Prioritization patterns

In contrast to the deferral patterns, these patterns consider what should be broken out and prioritized to be developed sooner.

- **Time-critical**: when external factors drive timing of work to be critical, consider what could be separated out that satisfies those needs, while not requiring all the work to be completed.

  Dante's announced they would be launching the ordering service in three months – they had to choose the minimum viable product that would keep that commitment.

- **Keep it simple first**: new work is always being uncovered – rather than adding to an existing PBI, keep the simplest option separate, and handle emerging work as new PBIs.

  Dante's initially added capabilities for extra toppings to the first ordering PBI, which became too big – they went back to the original PBI and added new PBIs instead.

- **Handling dependencies**: when multiple teams are working on the same product, consider handling the inter-dependencies by negotiating with another team to prioritize dependent work far earlier than they otherwise might have.

  If Dante's were to become part of a large retail food brand, they will likely share some services and need to liaise with other teams in order to launch or update their order system.

- **Major effort first**: when something is critical but requires a large amount of work, it is better do it earlier and remove any risk involved in delaying it and finding problems later.

  It doesn't matter which credit card Dante's choose to support first, as the first one will always take the most time.

- **Mitigating risk through additional research**: when there is high uncertainty – for example, the team cannot see what's needed or they are facing a new technology – run a Spike (see page 94) so that you can learn more, confirm what's feasible, provide a reference, and reassess the work.

  Although Dante's decided to defer development of a smartphone or tablet app, they did create a proof of concept that provided them with a reference they could use in later Sprints.

Don't forget

Work might become time critical due to regulatory change, service-level agreements, or market expectations.

Beware

While this breaks the independence principle of INVEST, this is a fact of life in large organizations.

65

Summary

- The Product Backlog is the prioritized requirements list for all functional development, fixes to the product, and enabling activities – collectively called Product Backlog Items (PBIs).

- Functional development is defined through Epics, Features, and Stories – Epics describe full end-to-end work flows, Features are the key capabilities required for an Epic, while Stories are the building blocks that make up the Features.

- Enabling activities covers Spikes, used to undertake research and prototyping, and any process improvements such as team improvements agreed at a Sprint Retrospective.

- The User Story is a common format for expressing requirements from an end-user perspective.

- To be well-formed, a PBI should meet the principles of INVEST – being independent, negotiable, valuable, estimatable, small enough, and testable.

- Acceptance Criteria define how the team will be able to tell if their work is acceptable – capturing what the product must and must not do – both functional and non-functional.

- Specification by example is a technique based on test-driven development that uses realistic examples to help make the Acceptance Criteria clearer.

- The Definition of Ready is a shared understanding by the Product Owner and the Delivery Team, regarding the preferred level of description that Product Backlog Items must have to be introduced at Sprint Planning.

- Backlog Refinement is an ongoing activity where the Product Owner works with the Discovery Team and Delivery Team to prepare the Product Backlog to meet the Definition of Ready.

- User Experience (UX) design provides more information for a PBI that helps describe how the customer is intended to interact with the product.

- When a PBI is too large to be completed in a single Sprint, it should be broken down – this chapter included 22 suggestions how.

5

Prioritizing and sizing the Backlog

A core agile value is responding to change over following a plan. With Scrum, planning happens far more frequently; the key difference is that it happens throughout the lifecycle rather than only up front.

Scrum maintains flexibility and mitigates risk with the principle of the *last responsible moment*. You should note, however, that the *last responsible moment* for something high-risk could be the first Sprint.

Five levels of agile planning

In feedback-driven development, responding to change is valued more than following a plan, but planning is still vital (see page 184). Rather than making detailed commitments up front, Scrum leaves commitment to the last responsible moment – planning iteratively and incrementally in more detail as the time horizon shortens.

The planning onion

At the highest level, planning starts with setting the Product Vision (covered in Chapter Three).

Early Discovery helps define a first cut of the high-level possible Features, as well as identifying potential risks and dependencies. From this, the Product Owner can derive their high-level Product Backlog and roughly plot out a Product Roadmap.

Ongoing Discovery, Refinement, and planning continues throughout and alongside Product Delivery, confirming the Features for each Release, pulling in the Product Backlog Items for each Sprint, and re-planning on a daily basis in the Daily Scrum to ensure the team will deliver a Product Increment.

These five levels of planning are reflected in a diagram known as the **planning onion**, due to its arrangement of concentric circles. This prompts for planning at each and every level of development.

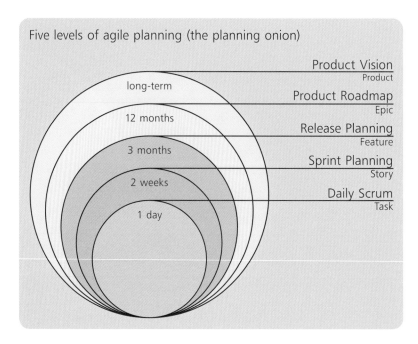

Five levels of agile planning (the planning onion)

The Product Roadmap

With a Product Vision in place, the Product Owner will have worked with their Discovery Team to identify the Features that will deliver the functionality required for all the customer journeys and workflows, and realize the vision and value they envisioned.

Product Delivery takes place over a period of time and will often involve a number of Releases. Where this spans many months, it helps the team if the Product Owner is able to provide visibility into the potential future direction of the product.

The Product Roadmap provides the ability to visualize likely capabilities required at key points in time over a long-range planning horizon. An example from Dante's below:

Release:	18.2	18.3	18.4	19.1
Goal:	Grow reach	Increase revenue	Mobile ordering	The big push
Features:	Online ordering Multiple items Pay on delivery	Suggest combo Pay online Menu admin	Basic app Discounts Delivery alerts	Smartphone and tablet app Build your own Driver tracker
Measures:	% online vs phone	Avg. order size	App downloads # orders	% app vs online No walk-ins

Timeline
The Discovery Team should identify the timing for potential Releases. These will be dependent on your marketing needs, but typically are no further apart than every three months.

Goals and Epics per Release
In determining what might be included in each Release, you should ideally plan forward from the Minimum Viable Product (see page 70), with each subsequent Release incrementally adding capabilities toward the envisioned complete product. It can be tempting to work backwards from an ideal product completion date. However, this encourages a more plan-driven approach and discourages acting on feedback.

Metrics
In adopting a feedback-driven framework for product development, you should define what to measure once the product is released. There should be a target for each measure, so you can demonstrate whether or not you have met the goal.

The Minimum Viable Product

A Product Owner will often prefer releasing to market only when the product does everything they want. Unfortunately, no matter how much analysis is done up front, it is rarely right first time.

Waiting for the full product to be ready increases costs and risks that the product may not meet customers' needs. It is better to get something into the customers' hands, and have them use it and provide feedback. This is faster and cheaper and allows the product to be adjusted earlier in its development.

To benefit from this approach, Product Owners must be able to identify and prioritize the **Minimum Viable Product** (MVP) required to be able to deliver some value and validate their idea.

Identifying the MVP

1 Choose which persona (see page 40) would best qualify as an early adopter for the product

2 Identify their critical job to be done and the minimum functionality which would achieve it (see page 38)

3 Consider whether anything can be removed and still achieve the job to be done – see Story Splitting (see page 60)

4 Define how to validate whether the MVP is successful

Techniques for identifying the MVP

Three effective techniques for identifying the MVP are:

- **Impact mapping**: visualizes the whole product scope, including personas, their jobs to be done, and the deliverables that should help them achieve that (see page 42).

- **Story mapping**: visualizes the steps and functionality for a single workflow (see page 57), which helps to identify the **Minimum Marketable Features** (MMF).

- **MoSCoW method**: each Product Backlog Item should be assessed for whether it is *Must have*, *Should have*, *Could have*, or *Won't have*. The MVP is represented by *Must have* Epics, while the MMF is all *Must have* Features within the MVP.

Hot tip

Minimum Lovable Product is an alternative to MVP, which stresses that the product should still provide a good customer experience, not just bare bones functionality.

Don't forget

While these techniques can be used separately, for best effect use *Story Mapping* to explore the detail in a workflow identified through *Impact Mapping*.

70

Prioritization

One of the Product Owner's key responsibilities is to ensure that the Product Backlog is refined and ready for Sprint Planning. For this they will need to identify which Product Backlog Items are the best candidates for the next Sprint.

Criteria for Prioritizing

Prioritizing PBIs will be influenced by a number of criteria:

- **Business Value**: in order to determine what Features will provide the most value the soonest, the Product Owner must ensure the team understands the value of each Feature.

- **Technical Debt**: teams should prioritize anything that stops the product from working, or blocks them from working on the items the Product Owner has selected for them.

- **Retiring risk early**: anything the team deems to be more uncertain or complex is worth resolving earlier – if it takes longer than expected, this doesn't come as a late surprise.

- **Clearing dependent work**: whenever work is identified as dependent on other work being completed first, that must influence the priority in which the other work is done.

- **Testing a hypothesis**: where the Product Owner is testing the water with an idea, they will need to get early feedback – this enables them to make decisions about further work.

- **Clearing the backlog**: anything that has been a low priority for a long time should be reassessed – take it back through the discovery process or consider discarding it altogether.

Striking a balance

While it is hard to decide which Features are more important, prioritizing too simplistically, such as classing 80% of the Product Backlog as *Must have*, helps nobody identify what to do next.

On the other hand, rather than attempting to prioritize the whole Product Backlog, the team only needs to focus on what they need to deliver in the next few Sprints.

The techniques on the following pages strike a balance between over-simplification and over-thinking. The right combination will depend on your organization and team – so it is best to explore these early on and agree on the balance that works for you.

Keep prioritization as objective possible. As it drives where we spend money, it can become influenced by politics, favors, or whoever shouts the loudest.

Prioritizing for flow of value

Without a rigorous approach behind it, prioritization can become too subjective. Stakeholders are often asked to force rank Epics and Features based on the order in which they feel each should be built. This often leads to conflict and risks giving way to the *highest-paid person's opinion* (the HiPPO).

To avoid these challenges, you need to adopt a more objective queuing model. This could be by prioritizing shorter work first, or by prioritizing work that delivers higher value first.

Shortest duration first

Prioritizing on the amount of effort will lead to completing some work earlier, which is more effective than completing work in the order it is requested (first in first out, FIFO). See the comparison below, where the shaded area represents the lost opportunity:

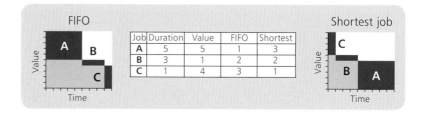

Job	Duration	Value	FIFO	Shortest
A	5	5	1	3
B	3	1	2	2
C	1	4	3	1

Highest value first

Alternatively, prioritizing by potential value will lead to releasing the work that will generate the greatest return first. When considering value, there are a number of factors:

- **Business Value**: the value of the work in the eyes of the organization or their customers, such as revenue growth, customer acquisition, or cost reduction (see page 78).

- **Time criticality**: the need to deliver something in a specific timescale, such as avoiding potential loss of earnings, meeting a key market event, or being ready for a new technology.

- **Operational value**: the long-term value to the organization – improving workflow, retiring risks early, or building capability – also known as *risk reduction and opportunity enablement*.

Collectively these are known as the **Cost of Delay** – a term meant to reflect what we lose if we delay Release, but can also be thought of as what we gain by releasing early.

While prioritizing by value is still more effective than FIFO queuing, it often results in delays before the first value is released. A better model would balance these two perspectives.

Balancing value and duration

In the **Weighted Shortest Job First** formula (WSJF), this better model divides the total cost of delay – the business, time criticality, and operational values – by the duration.

$$\text{WSJF} = \frac{\text{Business Value} + \text{Time Criticality} + \text{Operational Value}}{\text{Duration}}$$

WSJF is also known as *Cost of Delay Divided by Duration* (or *CD3*).

Based on this relative calculation, work of similar value will be prioritized based on what can be delivered faster, while work of similar duration will be prioritized by what delivers more value.

This model implicitly encourages teams to break down their work and to discard functionality with little value.

When comparing the relative degree of lost opportunity, WSJF is twice as effective as prioritizing on highest value or shortest duration alone, and is three times as effective compared with FIFO.

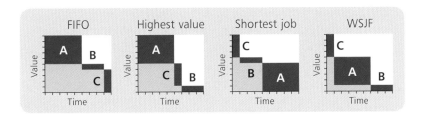

Calculating these factors to any level of precision, however, is time-consuming and unlikely to yield sufficient benefit for the additional effort. Instead, you could approximate these factors with points from the Fibonacci scale – as described in terms of Business Value (see page 78) and size (see page 74).

Substituting points into each factor of the WSJF formula gives rise to the **Value Flow Rate** model. Overall, this approach shifts the conversation to focus on throughput of value rather than on economic estimates and prioritization.

While *Value Flow Rate* and *WSJF* provide a more balanced priority, they are best used with points, or only at the Epic level, due to the effort involved in calculations.

Assessing size, not effort

Experience of working on product development has shown that human beings are inherently flawed when it comes to estimating time or cost, especially when developing novel products.

The only time we know how long something will take is after it has been completed. There is little point in investing too much time up front to calculate detailed estimates that will be wrong.

Comparing rather than estimating

Humans are, however, excellent at comparison. We evolved the ability to assess quickly whether animals were faster than us and if they could be a threat or a meal. As a modern example, we are able to assess comparative speed so we know when it is safe to cross the road, even though we cannot determine precise speed.

It is better to be roughly right than precisely wrong. When it comes to planning our work, it is better to work with abstractions. The most common ones are **Story points** and **T-shirt sizes**.

Story points

Product Backlog Items such as Stories, are usually sized with Story points. This is based on the Fibonacci sequence – in which each number is the sum of the two preceding numbers – 1, 2, 3, 5, 8, 13, 21, 34, 55, 89, etc. This *wideband Delphi* sequence is useful; as the gap between the numbers increases, this forces the decision to use one in preference to another. In adopting this for Story points, however, the sequence has been rounded off:

1, 2, 3, 5, 8, 13, then 20, 40, and 100.

T-shirt sizes

Larger bodies of work – such as major Epics and Features – are typically sized in a more abstract form. The most common is T-shirt sizes, as the abbreviations of S, M, L and XL are widely known.

Size is dependent on team

When a team assesses the size of a PBI, they are doing so based on the experience of working together, their familiarity with the technology involved, and their understanding of what is required.

As each team is made up of different people, the same piece of work will often be sized differently between teams. This is OK, as size rarely needs to be compared across teams.

Hot tip

Experienced teams often drop size 2 – forcing more of a choice between 1 and 3.

Beware

Do not try to compare Story points between teams, except when multiple teams are working on the same Product Backlog (see Chapter Ten).

How size relates to time

Size should not be used as a measure of time, as it encompasses the three complementary concerns of complexity, risk, and effort.

By acknowledging that we cannot know everything before work starts, and using an abstract measure to size the work, we accept and absorb the variability that arises. For example, a three-point Story might take two days on average to complete. However, do not take this to mean that you can forecast that all three-point Stories will take two days. The actual time to complete a three-point Story will be distributed along a curve. This can even mean that at times, some lower point-sized work will take longer than some higher point-sized work. While rare, this is perfectly normal.

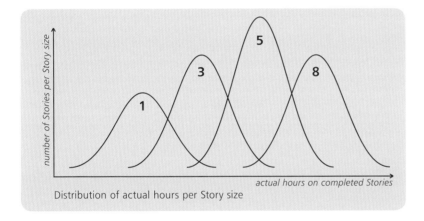

Distribution of actual hours per Story size

Organizations should keep metrics on average time to complete each size Story to identify changing trends. If it increases, the team might need coaching or training. If it decreases, on the other hand, this might mean the team are improving enough to consider recalibrating how they size. High-performing teams that are reliably breaking Product Backlog Items down into similar-sized work may be able to dispense with sizing altogether.

Just as with Story points, while T-shirt sizes are not time-based, you still need to make sense of roughly determining how long a large body of work would take. For this reason, you can create a conversion rate from abstract sizes to number of Sprints. For example, a small T-shirt size might be thought of as roughly equivalent to a half-Sprint, a medium to a full Sprint, a large to three Sprints, and an extra-large to five Sprints or more.

Sizing by affinity

When a team is newly formed or faces a new technology, they do not have a history of delivering work of this type together. That makes it much harder for them to assess the relative size of new Product Backlog Items (PBIs).

The **Affinity Sizing Game** – or Bockman Technique, after its creator Steve Bockman – enables a team to review and compare PBIs, grouping those of similar size together.

To prepare for Affinity Sizing

To play this game, you need all PBIs on cards or cut-up sheets in a pile that everyone can easily access. You will also need a clear table or wall, re-usable adhesive putty, sticky-notes, and marker pens.

The game is mostly played in silence, to avoid anyone overly influencing others in the team.

The game is played in two rounds: firstly, the team groups PBIs based on relative complexity, risk, and effort. In the second part, they assign a relative size (number of Story points) to each group.

Comparing relative complexity, risk, and effort

In the first part of the game, the goal is to have all PBIs arranged left-to-right – in order of relative size, smallest to largest.

1. First person takes the PBI from the top of the pile and places it centrally on the table or wall

2. Second person takes the next PBI from the pile and positions it relative to the one already on the table or wall – smaller to the left, larger to the right, same underneath

3. Next person chooses from one of the following actions:

   - Take the next PBI and place it relative to others

   - Move a PBI already placed to a new position

   - Pass (skip a turn)

4. Repeat Step 3 until all PBIs have been placed and nobody wants to move one of the PBIs already placed (i.e. everyone has passed)

Affinity grouping can also be used to rapidly form a consensus on Business Value or other attributes of a PBI.

To avoid distraction, put any PBIs to one side that are repeatedly moved back and forth. These are *outliers* to be discussed another time.

Assigning relative size

In the second part of the game, the goal is to assign a Story point size for the PBIs. Start by preparing a set of sticky-notes with one number each from the Story point sequence:

1, 2, 3, 5, 8, 13, 20, 40, and 100.

5 First person looks at the left-most PBI and considers whether this is likely to represent the smallest size – based on that, they choose the sticky-note for 1, 2, or 3 and place it above the first PBI

6 Next person chooses from one of the following actions:

- Take the sticky-note for the next size up and place it above the first PBI they feel represents a step up in complexity, risk, or effort – or create a blank space and place the sticky-note above that if they feel nothing is that size

- Move a sticky-note already placed to the left or right, above an alternative PBI they feel better represents that size

- Pass (skip a turn)

7 Repeat Step 6 until all sticky-notes have been placed and nobody wants to move one (i.e. everyone has passed)

All PBIs from one sticky-note up to the next are then assigned the Story points of that sticky-note. An example result below:

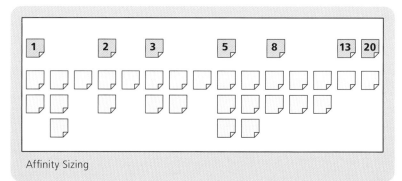

Affinity Sizing

Assessing Business Value

Business Value means different things to different organizations. Traditionally, a commercial organization's first priority has been to return a dividend to shareholders, while perhaps government agencies have statutory obligations as their primary objective.

Increasingly, organizations are taking the impact on people and the planet into account, as well as profit. In an age of constant digital disruption and customers ever more willing to switch their allegiance, the quality of service and the customer experience are also becoming stronger criteria.

The mix that makes up Business Value will vary by organization, with some examples given below. The Product Owner should spend time with their Discovery Team, and other stakeholders, to agree a definition of what they mean by Business Value.

Whatever the combination, the work that contributes most to those drivers should be prioritized ahead of that which doesn't. Rather than estimating value in virtual dollars, this focuses instead on what the work is intended to achieve for the organization, shifting the mindset from what it costs to what it gains.

Examples of Business Value drivers

- **Increase revenue**: to make more money, raise more taxes, or increase sponsorship and donations.

- **Protect revenue**: to retain customers or fight off competition.

- **Avoid or reduce costs**: to streamline operations, introduce efficiencies in the value stream, or reduce Technical Debt.

- **Improve customer experience**: to ensure that products and services meet the needs of real customers and to enable a service experience that meets expectation or even delights.

- **Meet regulatory and social obligations**: to do the right thing legally, ethically, and socially; to protect the organization from risk of fines, bad press, or losing key leadership.

- **Achieve market strategy**: to build brand recognition, grow market share, or implement a Product Roadmap.

- **Develop staff**: to recruit and retain the best people, train and develop them to be the best they can be, and support them with appropriate remuneration and benefits.

Determining Business Value

It is one thing to identify work that should contribute to your organization's strategic goals or drivers. It is harder to express this in a way that is comparable and therefore useful for prioritization.

You could choose to invest in calculating the financial impact of any work. This could be used to drive a higher priority for higher value work. However, while this might be possible for every Epic, it would likely be too time-consuming to do for every Feature and Story on the Product Backlog.

The Business Value Game

Discovery Teams can choose to score Business Value rather than calculate detailed values for every single Epic, Feature, and Story. This is called the **Business Value Game**, a variant of the Affinity Sizing Game (see page 76). To avoid confusion with Story points, some organizations make their Business Value range much higher:

100, 200, 300, 500, 800, 1200, 2000, 5000.

As with Story points, the gap between each Business Value widens as the numbers increase. This, again, is to force an active decision to choose one over another.

There is no direct correlation between these numbers and any potential earnings or savings in dollars. This is intended to be a simple model that enables the Discovery Team to compare Business Value and assess which PBIs are more valuable.

Business Value is dynamic

Once the Product Backlog has had its value assessed in this way, it should not be treated as a static statement of value. Rather, as Features are released and feedback is received, the Business Value for remaining work could change as certain Features may become more or less attractive.

Don't forget

Feedback could be qualitative (e.g. social media posts, app store ratings, survey responses) or quantitative (e.g. revenue in dollars, number of transactions, growth in active users).

Release Planning

The Product Vision provides the True North for developing or enhancing a product. The Product Roadmap provides the high-level view of how the product's Features will be released over time.

Organizations that have adopted Scrum should be capable of releasing Product Increments at the end of a Sprint. In many organizations, however, there is an overhead in integrating work before it can be released. Sometimes the Product Owner may choose to wait until they have enough Features to release together.

While not formally a part of Scrum, this is handled through the Release cycle, an additional level of planning between the Roadmap and Sprints. This takes the Epics that have been road-mapped for a Release and roughly maps the corresponding Features and Stories across a number of Sprints.

The Release is planned against a single constraint, either to determine how much scope can be delivered in a fixed number of Sprints or how many Sprints it will take to deliver a fixed scope.

To run a successful Release Planning session, ensure all the right people are invited, that they have been briefed adequately beforehand, that the space has been set up, and all the materials should be prepared and at hand.

Inviting the right people

As with Product Discovery, a range of stakeholders should be involved, including key customer-facing, operational, and technical roles. In Release Planning, the whole Delivery Team should also be involved. This helps them gain a common understanding of the work and to start bonding if they are a new team.

Space and material for Release Planning

The Release Planning session needs to be booked in a large open space with a blank wall and a large table.

The wall or table should be prepared with masking tape to mark off columns for each Sprint. Where more than one team is involved, there should also be rows marked off per team.

All Feature PBIs intended for that Release should be piled in priority order on the table. There should also be blank index cards, marker pens and re-usable adhesive putty.

Beware

If both scope and time are fixed in advance then it is not an agile project and the team needn't have the overhead of using Scrum.

The Release Planning process

Repeat the following steps until the planning constraint is met:

1 Start by taking the first few Feature PBIs from the pile

2 For each Feature PBI:

- Consider what might be required to implement it
- Assign a T-shirt size to it
- If it is larger than a medium, split it into Story PBIs on index cards (see Chapter Four)

3 Repeat Step 2 until the Sprint is full

4 Stick the first Sprint's PBIs on the wall

When there is a fixed number of Sprints, Steps 1-4 are repeated until every Sprint for the Release has PBIs. This shows how much scope will be delivered for that number of Sprints.

When there is a fixed scope, Steps 1-4 are repeated until all the PBIs in that scope have been stuck to the wall. This shows how many Sprints it will take to deliver that much scope.

How to handle the Release Plan giving the wrong answer

Sometimes, you may feel the Release Plan does not represent a good return on investment or that the desired scope is too expensive. It can be tempting to ask the team to re-size to fit, but this tends to hide problems that will surface again later.

Instead, the Product Owner should review the Release Plan with the team, and together they should consider the following:

- Split out less important elements from each Feature and add them to the Product Backlog as new PBIs for later delivery.

- Choose a simpler solution and add PBIs to the Product Backlog to make it more sophisticated later.

- Identify any Risks, Dependencies, or Assumptions and what could be done to resolve these.

Hot tip

As this exercise is still at a relatively high level, it is recommended to use more abstract sizing, such as T-shirt sizes.

Beware

Challenging the team on their sizing can demotivate them and discourage the self-organization that makes Scrum so successful.

Summary

- To keep commitment to the last responsible moment, Scrum adopts the five levels of agile planning; from the Product Vision at the highest level, through the Product Roadmap, Release Planning and Sprint Planning, to the Daily Scrum.

- These planning levels correspond to Product Backlog Items: the Roadmap is planned around Epics, the Release maps Features to Sprints, the Sprint commits to Stories for those Features, and each day is spent on Tasks for those Stories.

- The Product Roadmap is designed to provide visibility for which capabilities the Product Owner expects, or would like to release at key times over a 12 or 18 month period – typically once per quarter.

- The team should work with the Product Owner to identify what is the Minimum Viable Product to include in each Release that will deliver value to the customer, realize benefits for the organization, and provide feedback for the team.

- The Minimum Viable Product is made up of *Must have* Epics, while the Minimum Marketable Features are all the Features that are *Must have* within the Minimum Viable Product.

- Teams should strive to include some *Should have* and even *Could have* Features per Release – as these are often factors that delight customers – but not so much as to risk delays.

- Until a team can reliably break down their work to create a flow of smaller items, it is important that they assess the size of their work, so that they can stop making them too large.

- To be able to prioritize the work, the Product Owner should assess the Business Value the organization expects to gain.

- Keep prioritization objective with a technique like Weighted Shortest Job First – which takes into account the potential value, the urgency, and the size of the work.

- When an organization does not deploy their work every Sprint, they need an additional orchestration cycle – called the Release – to organize the work of multiple Sprints.

- Each Release starts with a Release Planning Event.

6 Preparing for the Sprint

With the work to build the product defined, prioritized, and sized in the Product Backlog, this chapter explores how the Delivery Team get started with development.

Getting ready to Sprint

Previous chapters covered forming a team, creating a vision for a product, forming the Product Backlog of everything required to build the product, then prioritizing and sizing the work. Now, the Delivery Team is ready to start work on that.

As an iterative approach to product development, the key is deciding how long the iterations should last. In some agile frameworks, such as Feature-Driven Development, the duration of each iteration fluctuates depending on the size of the Features being developed. In Scrum, on the other hand, the iteration is a fixed time-box known as the Sprint.

In each Sprint, the Product Owner and the team select the top priority work, break it down so that it can be completed within a single Sprint, and then work together through the Sprint to deliver a good-quality, usable, and potentially shippable increment of the product.

Deciding on the duration of the Sprint

While the Scrum Guide advises a duration of one month or shorter, in practice there have been Sprints of six weeks and longer. This is rare, and usually caused by significant external dependencies – see Organizational Impediments (see page 150).

The duration for your Sprint is determined by a number of factors, for example how often the team is able to show and release their work in a reliably finished state.

The team needs to complete any work they start within a single Sprint. The work needs to be broken down to be small enough, and the Sprint itself needs to be long enough for everything critical to be completed so that it can be released.

- Teams working on new products will have few dependencies and be more likely to choose a Sprint of one week.

- Teams working on well-established products will have a number of complex integration points and be more likely to choose Sprints of three or four weeks.

- The most common duration for a Sprint is two weeks.

The team at Dante's, our pizza takeaway business, has considered the options and chosen the standard duration of two weeks.

Sprint duration should be consistent

Once a Sprint duration has been chosen, it is critical that all Sprints should be of the same length.

This consistency makes the process repeatable and allows the team to establish a rhythm (sometimes referred to as the *cadence*, *pulse* or *heartbeat* of Scrum). This allows the team to forecast how many Story points they can typically complete in a single Sprint (also known as their *Velocity*).

To help the team establish that rhythm, the Sprint is made up of a series of key events (sometimes called *ceremonies*). Each Sprint starts with Sprint Planning and ends with a Sprint Review and Sprint Retrospective. Every day during the Sprint there is a Daily Scrum, alongside the development of the product itself.

An exception to the fixed duration could be over the Christmas holidays – most of the team is likely to be away from work for some or all of two weeks. At this time, the duration is often stretched to include additional elapsed weeks sufficient to achieve a similar number of working hours for the team. So, a two-week Sprint could stretch to three or even four weeks.

Canceling a Sprint

There should be no gap between Sprints; a new Sprint starts immediately after the end of the preceding one. Once a Sprint has started it should continue until the end of the allotted time.

However, should the Sprint goal become obsolete, the Product Owner may decide to cancel the Sprint. For example:

- The organization changes strategy

- The chosen technology is replaced

- New legislation is suddenly enacted

Even then, a Sprint would only be canceled if the resulting Product Increment would be discarded. Given the short duration of Sprints, it is extremely rare that a Sprint is canceled.

Should this happen, the Product Owner could choose to accept any potentially reusable work that has been completed. Any Product Backlog Items that were incomplete or not started would be put back on the Product Backlog.

Don't forget

While Sprints should always be of the same duration, some organizations choose to extend them over the Christmas holidays.

Beware

Sprints should only be canceled if the work that would be completed would be discarded.

Sprint Planning

Early on in product development, planning is kept at a high-level because much can change as feedback is obtained. The Product Vision defines the purpose for developing a product; the Product Roadmap provides a view of how Features in the product will be released over time; and the Release Plan roughly maps out how the functionality for each Feature will be developed over a given number of Sprints (typically up to six).

In Scrum, it is not until Sprint Planning that the team commits to the work they plan to deliver in that Sprint.

Working collaboratively with the Product Owner, the team select a subset of Product Backlog Items (PBIs) that they agree can be completed within a single Sprint. They then determine the Tasks required to successfully deliver those PBIs. This committed list of PBIs and Tasks becomes the Sprint Backlog.

Before you begin
In order to run Sprint Planning, you will need a **Ready Backlog** of Product Backlog Items that have been:

- Prioritized by the Product Owner (see page 71), as the best functionality to build next.

- Seen and refined in advance by the team, meaning there are no surprises and the team have been able to ask questions.

- Agreed as meeting their Definition of Ready (see page 53).

Attendees
Sprint Planning is a collaborative effort between the Product Owner (who clarifies the PBIs and their Acceptance Criteria), the Delivery Team (who define the work and effort required to complete the agreed PBIs), and the Scrum Master (who facilitates the event).

Timing
Sprint Planning is the first activity at the start of each Sprint. The team needs to allow enough time to select the PBIs they want to work on in the coming Sprint and plan the corresponding Tasks.

For a standard two-week Sprint, they should allow up to four hours – pro-rata for Sprints of a different duration – that is, two hours per week.

The Sprint Backlog

The Sprint Backlog is the set of Product Backlog Items (PBIs) that have been selected for a Sprint, together with the Tasks planned for how to deliver each PBI.

It is the Delivery Team's forecast of the functionality that they will be building into the next Product Increment, together with the work effort needed to deliver it.

A visible picture of the work

The Sprint Backlog acts as a visible picture of the work that the Delivery Team plans to complete during the Sprint. It often takes on a physical form, such as a Scrum Board (see page 100), where the team put up cards or sticky-notes to show what work has to be done. Increasingly it is digital, using one of the many agile management tools available. However, even when digital, it is typically displayed in a similar layout to the Scrum Board.

Measuring progress through the Sprint

The PBIs, the Tasks to deliver those PBIs, and the hours estimated per Task are all used to help measure and track progress throughout the Sprint.

Many teams view their plan for the Sprint on a Scrum Board (physical or digital), and reflect progress by moving the Tasks across as the status changes until they are all done.

As the team works on each Task, the number of hours remaining is reduced, so the total number of hours steadily reduces toward a target of zero by the end of the Sprint. This progressive reduction is called *burning down*.

Changing the Sprint Backlog

The Sprint Backlog should have sufficient detail in the plan to allow progress to be monitored against it. As the Delivery Team complete Tasks, they will learn more about the work required. This may result in some new Tasks being identified, and some existing Tasks no longer being needed.

While the team should not be adding or removing PBIs in the Sprint Backlog after a Sprint has started, they can and should add or remove Tasks to ensure the plan for the Sprint is still relevant and accurate.

There are many digital agile management tools, from basic board tools like *Trello*, *Scrumwise*, or *Kanbanery*, to full planning and tracking tools like *Jira*, *VersionOne*, and *Team Foundation Server*.

Definition of Done

As Delivery Teams work through their Sprint Backlog, they need a clear way of understanding and communicating when each Product Backlog Item (PBI) is **Done**. Left to the individual, the meaning of Done can be highly subjective. Perhaps they are finished with their part and someone else needs to do something, such as a programmer wanting a tester to take it over.

The PBI is only really Done when it is ready to be integrated into the full product, which can then be released or launched without requiring further work. What is required for this will differ from organization to organization, from product to product, and even from team to team.

Defining what Done means

To make this clear to everyone, especially members of the team, the meaning of this is captured in a Definition of Done. The Definition of Done acts as a checklist of activities or deliverables that must be completed for the PBI to be classed as Done.

The Definition of Done has to include everything critical the team needs to do in order to be confident that their work is fit for purpose. As such, it acts as *exit criteria* for the team's work.

Creating a Definition of Done

Teams often create their Definition of Done by brainstorming, where the whole team tries to think of everything that might be needed. Unfortunately this is often insufficient.

There will always be organizational constraints that the team has to meet, such as architectural standards, development guidelines, quality processes, and even regulation and social concerns.

A well-formed Definition of Done should not just encompass what the team believes to be necessary and known organizational constraints, but should also take into account the needs of those to whom they are delivering the product.

This includes the needs of the sales, support, and billing teams. It may also include the needs of other teams involved in integrating, assuring, and launching the product.

As well as using the Definition of Done during Sprint Planning, teams often post this up somewhere prominent near their workspace.

As this was Dante's first Sprint, they brainstormed what they thought should be in a Definition of Done, example below:

<u>Dante's Definition of Done</u>

- *Deliverables reviewed and meet QA, Dev, and BA standards*
- *Source code is checked in to the repository*
- *Analytics are built-in and capturing usage statistics*
- *Any un-implemented features are hidden in the product*
- *Deliverables are fully integrated and the build is release-ready*
- *Documentation is complete*
- *Testing is complete*
- *All automated tests are in the framework and are passing*

- *Performance and security testing completed or agreed 'out of cycle'*
- *Deliverables demonstrated to the Product Owner*
- *Meets all Acceptance Criteria, including examples*
- *No outstanding Bugs: no Sev-1 or Sev-2 at all, and any Sev-3 or Sev-4 have been closed or elevated to Defects at Product Owner's discretion*
- *The team is ready to demonstrate this in the Sprint Review*
- *Product Owner has approved that everything needed has been done*

The benefits of the Definition of Done

- Collaborating on the Definition of Done helps the team bond together – it helps them focus on what they jointly aim to achieve each Sprint, rather than on their own specialism.

- A well-formed Definition of Done is good for removing ambiguity when communicating with stakeholders, and helps to reduce risk – when the team says they are Done, everyone will know what this means.

- Lastly, it helps the team stay focused – in Sprint Planning, by using this as a reference, the guesswork is removed and the team can focus on Delivery.

Inspect and adapt

As with other aspects of how the team works, the Definition of Done is not cast in concrete. It should be revised as needed.

Typically, after each Sprint, as the team holds their retrospective, they will consider whether anything was missed or done unnecessarily. If it was critical or happens repeatedly, the team should consider updating their Definition of Done accordingly.

Building the Sprint Backlog

The first step in Sprint Planning is for the team to select those Product Backlog Items (PBIs) that they agree they would be capable of completing in a single Sprint.

Agreeing a goal for the Sprint

Just as the product itself has a high-level Product Vision, so too does each Sprint need a goal. The purpose of the Sprint goal is to help orient the team toward whatever is most critical as an outcome for the Sprint.

Sometimes, the Product Owner will have such a clear vision of what they would like from the team that they can articulate a clear Sprint goal at the beginning of Sprint Planning.

It is more common, however, that the Product Owner waits to see what the team is able to commit to, which often follows some negotiation and work breakdown, and then crafts a Sprint goal that encompasses the majority of that.

However, the team will benefit more from a clearly defined goal. While it may be easier to make a Sprint goal from what is in the Sprint Backlog, this often results in a long and awkwardly-worded goal that the team cannot easily use for orientation.

Adjusting Target Velocity

The team will know how many Story points they have been able to complete for each of the last three Sprints. The average Story points across those Sprints is known as the Velocity, and is an important measure when planning an upcoming Sprint.

Where the team will be missing key people for some or all of the upcoming Sprint, the Target Velocity used for Planning should be adjusted down proportionally.

For example, the team at Dante's has eight members; so if two of them will be out for the whole Sprint – for training or annual leave, for example – their Velocity should be reduced by 25%.

Selecting Stories into the Sprint Backlog

The Product Owner will come prepared with a pile of Story PBIs, in a priority order they feel reflects the importance of new capabilities they will provide customers, the value they will earn the organization, or the feedback they will generate.

For each Story in the pile, in order of priority:

1 The Product Owner presents the Story

2 The team asks questions to refresh their understanding so they have confidence they can plan the Tasks required

3 If the Story does not meet the team's Definition of Ready (see Chapter Four), the Product Owner may ask them to undertake a Spike (see page 94) to find out more

4 If the Story is Ready, the team size it in Story points, based on the complexity, risk, and effort

5 If the Story is larger than their nominal maximum (e.g. 13 Story points), they work together to split it into a few smaller Stories which are added to the Product Backlog

6 If the team agrees they can complete the Story in a single Sprint, and have enough Velocity left, they add it to the Sprint Backlog pile and add the Story points to a running tally – otherwise it should be held back for the next Backlog Refinement or Sprint Planning session

The above steps are repeated until the running tally of Story points exceeds that Sprint's Target Velocity by a small margin.

Keep the Sprint Backlog achievable
Teams often want additional Stories ready, in case they complete their Sprint Backlog early. Known as **Stretch** Stories, these should be marked as Ready, but kept in the Product Backlog. This ensures committed work is completed before anything new is started.

When you have no historical Velocity
New teams have no past Sprints to calculate their Velocity. They should choose an arbitrary number as a Target Velocity. This can still be adjusted when the work is planned out at the Task level.

The team at Dante's chose a Target Velocity of 50. From this, they chose seven PBIs (six at five Story points each, and one at 20).

The team will have already seen these PBIs during Backlog Refinement (see page 55).

When new Stories are created during Sprint Planning, consider only the highest priority ones for that Sprint.

91

Planning Poker

In Chapter Five we saw how teams can size Product Backlog Items (PBIs) with the Affinity Sizing Game. That approach is based on a team grouping together PBIs of similar complexity, risk, and effort in order to assess their relative size in Story points. Affinity Sizing is a useful technique when teams have not been working long together or are dealing with a new technology.

However, when teams are considering PBIs similar to the ones they have already been delivering over a number of Sprints, they will have a benchmark against which to assess relative size. **Planning Poker** is an alternative game which is faster at assessing the relative size of an individual PBI.

Like many other techniques used with Scrum, *Planning Poker* originated with Extreme Programming (see page 105).

When to use Planning Poker

Planning Poker is typically used when selecting PBIs during Sprint Planning (see page 90). The team has to size a Story before confirming they can complete it in the upcoming Sprint. For experienced teams, it can also be used while refining the Product Backlog in place of Affinity Sizing.

The Planning Poker cards

The name **Planning Poker** is derived from the way team members select a card from their hand, and reveal it at the same time. These numbered cards are based on the Story point range (see Chapter Five):

1, 2, 3, 5, 8, 13, 20, 40, and 100.

These are often extended by cards with the following symbols:

0 The zero indicates an insignificant amount of time that should not affect the team's Velocity.

? The question mark indicates there is not enough information to be able to assess the relative size.

∞ The infinity symbol indicates that the work is too large to assess, and must be broken down.

☕ The coffee cup indicates that the team member is tired and needs a break.

Planning Poker does not have to be conducted in silence. As the selected cards are revealed at the same time, the team avoids anchoring themselves around the first size that was mentioned.

How to play Planning Poker

Neither the Scrum Master nor the Product Owner play a hand – instead, they facilitate the session and explain what is required.

The Scrum Master ensures that each team member has a hand of cards. All hands have the same set of cards.

Then, for each Story being assessed:

Beware

The Product Owner should not have a say in the size as they will not be doing the work.

1 The Product Owner explains the Story

2 The team asks questions to clarify Risks or Dependencies

3 When the Scrum Master decides there has been enough discussion, they call on the team to size the Story

4 Each player individually selects a card from their hand that represents their estimate, and lays it on the table, face down so that their selection is hidden

5 Everyone turns over their cards at the same time

6 Anyone who has played a card much lower or higher than the average then explains why they selected those cards; why they believe the work to be simpler or more complex

7 If there is sufficient difference, the team cycles back to Step 2 and repeats until they reach a consensus or settle on a closely banded range; at which point they may agree to go with the higher size so that they can move on

8 Finally, if the team cannot reach agreement, the story is put back in the Product Backlog. The Product Owner might agree to a time-boxed Spike for someone in the team to find out more information, before the next Backlog Refinement session

Alternative to Planning Poker cards

Where Story point cards are not available, there are alternatives, such as using a standard card deck or a smartphone app.

Spikes reduce uncertainty

In refining and sizing a Product Backlog Item (PBI), the Product Owner and team will encounter many uncertainties and complexities. When there are too many to fully assess the potential solution, the PBI should be agreed as not ready for the Sprint.

Rather than putting pressure on the team to jump to a solution, the Product Owner should instead consider investing some time in the coming Sprint to undertake research, design, exploration, or prototyping. This is referred to as a **Spike**.

Unlike PBIs which add functionality to a Product Increment, the sole purpose of a Spike is to gain knowledge. The knowledge will improve understanding of requirements, or reduce the risk in specific technical options.

A Spike should be focused on a single well-articulated question or problem statement. Break a complex scenario into multiple Spikes, just as you would break down an over-sized PBI.

Functional Spike

When a team has uncertainty regarding how the customer would interact with their product, they undertake a functional Spike to analyze the overall functionality required, assess how to break it down, and consider where any risk and complexities lie.

For example, instead of committing themselves to the 20-point PBI, Karly, the Product Owner at Dante's, could have allowed the team a day to research ways that customers like to order pizza.

Technical Spike

When a team has uncertainty about the potential technical solution or the effort to build it, they undertake a technical Spike to research what options are feasible for the chosen technology. They might use this to compare potential performance loads of different solutions, to evaluate different tools or languages to use, or just generally to gain confidence with a technology.

For example, instead of committing themselves to PBIs for the smartphone app in their first Sprint, the Dante's team could have invested time in developing a Proof of Concept. Strictly speaking, anything developed as part of a Spike should be thrown away – although many teams retain their work as a reference build for future Sprints. Either way, this would still have helped the team to become familiar with the new technology.

Knowing when a Spike is Done

A Spike does not need to adhere to the team's Definition of Done as anything produced will normally be discarded after it has answered the question. Rather than being sized like a PBI, a Spike is time-boxed. The Product Owner will agree a number of hours to conduct the investigation, typically shorter than a day. The Spike ends when that number of hours has been used.

The Spike should generate one or more deliverables that help the Product Owner and team resolve whatever doubts or uncertainties they have. These could be an equivalent example from another team or organization, an improved workflow, or a throwaway prototype.

These deliverables are reviewed in the next Backlog Refinement session (see Chapter Four) to consider whether there is now enough information to size and plan the PBI in a future Sprint Planning session.

Including Spikes in the Sprint Backlog

Rather than treating a Spike like a PBI, it should instead be thought of as a Task for a PBI that is taking place in an earlier Sprint than the one in which it will itself be done. Spikes should be added to the Sprint Backlog and tracked on the team's Scrum Board with all the other Tasks.

As Spikes represent uncertainty in a PBI, planning the Spike and the PBI in the same Sprint is to be discouraged. However, if the uncertainty was low enough and the team reserved sufficient capacity, once the Spike has been completed, the team could agree to handle the related PBI in the same Sprint.

Use sparingly

By their very nature, every PBI involves some level of risk and unknowns; that's why Scrum is a feedback-driven framework. The full solution is progressively uncovered during Backlog Refinement, Sprint Planning, and in Sprint.

All these activities are minor forms of a Spike. The team will learn how to work collaboratively to resolve this uncertainty. Spikes should only be used for more critical or large uncertainties.

Beware

Unless you have reserved enough capacity, adding a PBI part-way through a Sprint is strongly discouraged.

Task planning for the Sprint

In the first step of Sprint Planning, the team built their Sprint Backlog, agreed on a Sprint goal and selected the Product Backlog Items (PBIs) they forecast could be completed in the next Sprint to meet that goal.

The next step for the team is to work out a detailed plan for how to deliver those Story PBIs. This will turn the forecast of Stories in their Sprint Backlog into a set of Tasks to which they can commit with confidence. This is vital, as *Commitment* is one of the core values of Scrum (see page 18).

Calculating the team's Capacity

The team's **Capacity** is the number of available hours they have to work in the Sprint. It can be thought of as their budget for the Sprint. The Capacity is calculated from three simple measures for each member of the team:

1 The number of Delivery hours in the work day: typically six or seven, to allow for disturbances such as general administration and company meetings

2 The number of days in the Sprint each person will be available: typically nine, one fewer than the number of days in a Sprint – to allow time for the Sprint Planning, Sprint Review, and Sprint Retrospective events – reduced further for any individuals with approved leave or training

3 The percentage of time they can dedicate to Delivery in that Sprint: typically 100%, but allow time for known responsibilities or activities outside the Sprint Backlog, such as production support or line management

As the team at Dante's is new, they have no responsibilities for production support or anything else outside their team. This means they will be dedicated full-time to the development. Nobody has any leave or training booked, so they calculate that their Sprint Capacity will be a little over 500 hours:

> 8 people @ 7 hours/day for 9 days = 504 hours

Planning the work for the Sprint

For the team to be confident that they can deliver the Stories they selected into the Sprint Backlog, they need to plan out the Tasks they will need to complete.

Tasks should include all the obvious activities, such as design, programming, and testing. In order to complete a Story there may be other deliverables that are required, such as release notes or customer training material. These would normally be captured in the Definition of Done (see page 88).

For reference, it is handy to have a copy of the team's Definition of Done to act as a checklist for each Story, to ensure they plan Tasks for all essential deliverables.

Identifying Tasks for each Story

Once the team is ready to plan what they need to do, they need the Stories they selected for their Sprint Backlog, their Sprint capacity, and each member of the team needs a pad of sticky-notes and a pen. The Product Owner does not strictly need to be involved in this step. However, if they leave after the first part of Sprint Planning, they should be available to answer questions if needed.

The team starts by writing out a sticky-note for each Spike and team improvement action they have agreed to complete in the upcoming Sprint. The number of hours agreed with the Product Owner is also written on the sticky-note. The total for all these time-boxed activities is subtracted from the team's capacity.

In order to deliver great products in Scrum, teams need a foundation of sound technical practices (see page 105).

...cont'd

Then, for each Story:

1 Someone reads out the description, Acceptance Criteria, and size

2 Each team member should focus on identifying as many Tasks as they can – for each Task they:

- Write one Task per sticky-note

- Call out the Task to the team

- Place the sticky-note in a pile for that Story

- Continue until no more Tasks are identified, which can take from 5-10 minutes per Story

3 The pile of sticky-notes is then arranged in a logical order. This can help spot gaps or duplicates to refine the Tasks created for a Story

4 Once the set of Tasks has been agreed, the team then estimate the hours per Task – this can be done by simply calling it out and writing it on the sticky-note to see if anyone disagrees. Alternatively, teams could use the Planning Poker approach, with the number on the card used to represent hours

5 The estimated hours for the whole Story are totaled and subtracted from the team's capacity identified earlier

The team considers whether they can sustainably take on more work. If they still have substantial capacity remaining, they then repeat Steps 1-5 for the next Story.

Once they get near their capacity, they should stop. Planning work for their full capacity leaves no margin for Tasks that are discovered once work starts.

Don't forget

Calling out each Task as it is created is a form of brainstorming, as this may prompt someone to think of other Tasks.

If this means that they cannot complete all the Stories they selected, they show the Product Owner which Stories need to be removed from the Sprint Backlog. If it is possible to break the remaining Stories into smaller items, the team can then plan them to establish whether they can take those on.

On rare occasions, the team might finish planning the work and realize that they still have significant spare capacity. They could consider any Stretch Stories they identified (see page 91). If the plan of work for a Stretch Story still fits within their capacity, then they could consider adding that to their Sprint Backlog.

After breaking the seven Stories into Tasks, the team at Dante's have a total of 300 hours estimated for their first Sprint.

Making Tasks SMART

While planning out the work to deliver each Story, the team should keep in mind that the Tasks they discuss and document should be **SMART** – an acronym that helps the team to remember that each Task should be:

- **Specific**: it should be unambiguous so that the whole team can understand what is needed. This might mean breaking larger activities into more than one Task.

- **Measurable**: it should be clear how the team can agree when the Task is Done. This is best achieved by defining Tasks in terms of their deliverables instead of just describing an activity.

- **Actionable**: it should be within the team's capabilities to deliver. Any Task that requires different skills or experiences should be mitigated or they could pair with a specialist outside the team in order to learn.

- **Relevant**: it should contribute to the Story being considered and nothing more. Any Task creating deliverables for something else should likely be under a different Story.

- **Time-boxed**: it should be small enough to be completed in less than a day. Any Task longer than six hours should likely be broken down.

Building the Scrum Board

Sprint Planning may take place over one or two sessions. Teams often benefit from a break after two hours of building their Sprint Backlog before they plan out their Tasks. Once they have finished Sprint Planning, the team should return to their team workspace and build their Scrum Board for that Sprint.

The Scrum Board

Delivery Teams track their work on a Scrum Board (also known as a *Task Board*, *Kanban Board*, or *Sprint Wall*).

In its simplest form, the Scrum Board can be a whiteboard or wall. With tape or marker pens, the board is divided into four columns:

PBI	To Do	In Progress	Done

Typical Scrum Board, at the start of a Sprint

Sticky-notes or index cards representing each PBI and Task are placed in the appropriate row and column, showing the status of work underway at any point in time.

While many organizations choose to vary the format, the team at Dante's are new to Scrum and chose to stick with this layout.

Benefits of a physical Scrum Board

Many teams manage their Scrum Board digitally, in an agile management tool, although maintaining a physical board also acts as:

- A big visible chart or *information radiator* – everyone in the team and their stakeholders can see what is happening.

- A focus point around which team members can gather to discuss their work, especially at their Daily Scrum event.

- A tactile representation of work in progress, where Tasks can be picked up, discussed, and re-attached in a different place – they can also be annotated with notes, color markers, and other signifiers to communicate additional information.

Geographically-dispersed teams typically rely more on an agile management tool. The recommendation is still that each local subset should maintain a physical Scrum Board as well.

Preparing the Scrum Board
Firstly, one or more team members should ensure the Scrum Board is ready to use:

- Any cards, sticky-notes and other information relating to the previous Sprint are removed and typically thrown away.

- Where a whiteboard is being used, any hand-written notes from the last Sprint are rubbed off.

Building the Sprint Backlog on the Scrum Board
The name of the Sprint and the Sprint goal is attached or written at the top of the Scrum Board. Then, working together, the team stick up the PBIs one below the other, in the order they should be completed. A horizontal line is drawn across to reserve a row per PBI. The top row is often kept free for any urgent work that arises through the Sprint, such as resolving a product defect.

All the Tasks identified in Sprint Planning are then stuck up in the **To Do** column, next to their PBI. Spikes and team improvements are stuck in an empty row at the bottom.

Selecting their first Tasks
Lastly, one-by-one the team should choose one Task each to start working on. They move that Task into the **In Progress** column.

Some teams choose to agree in advance who will do each Task, and in rare circumstances even permit a senior member of the team to assign Tasks to other team members. Both practices are discouraged as they reduce flexibility and autonomy. It is better to allow each team member to choose their own work. Where a team member is new, another member may assist their selection.

Using avatars to represent the Task owner
Most teams also indicate who is doing each Task, showing the rest of the team and their stakeholders who is doing what.

This can be done using a small sticker with the team member's name. However, most people illustrate themselves with an avatar, such as a cartoon character, which somehow represents them.

Beware

If someone consistently cherry-picks the more *interesting* work, the rest of the team should challenge that behavior.

Summary

- Teams need to choose a Sprint duration that best meets their needs to release early and often while working within their organizational constraints – two weeks is the typical duration.

- The Sprint duration should not be changed from one Sprint to the next – this constraint allows time for inspection and adaptation, encourages breaking work down into smaller pieces, and helps to improve the flow of work.

- Once a Sprint has started, it may be canceled early at the discretion of the Product Owner, but only when extenuating circumstances would render the Sprint goal irrelevant and any deliverables unusable – however, this should be rare.

- The Sprint starts with the Sprint Planning event, in which the team collaborates with the Product Owner on establishing a Sprint goal and a Sprint Backlog of work.

- Sprint Planning is time-boxed to four hours for a typical two-week Sprint – pro-rata lower or higher for shorter or longer Sprint durations.

- The Sprint goal is a short expression of the purpose of a Sprint; ideally the business problem that is to be addressed.

- The Sprint Backlog is a subset of Product Backlog Items – and the Tasks required to build them – that the team has forecast they will be able to complete within a single Sprint.

- The Definition of Done establishes a shared understanding of how the team will be able to confirm their work as complete with the Product Owner.

- Teams use Planning Poker to help assess when work needs to be broken down more if it cannot be completed in a single Sprint.

- The Product Owner can help the team to reduce risk and uncertainty by planning a Spike to investigate requirements or solutions – normally time-boxed to less than a day.

- The team confirm that they will be able to complete the forecast Sprint Backlog by planning the detailed Tasks needed to complete the work.

7 A day in the life of a Sprint

Up until now, the Product Owner and the team have selected what they can deliver, and planned their work. This chapter covers the activities the team does on a daily basis during the Sprint to build the product and get it ready to be released.

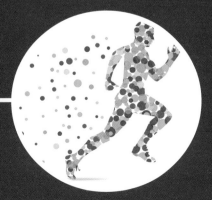

What happens in a Sprint

By now, the Scrum Team have progressively worked through four levels of agile planning: from developing the vision, creating a twelve-month Roadmap, creating a quarterly Release Plan, and selecting Product Backlog Items (PBIs) for their Sprint. Now, they are starting the work of building the product in the Sprint.

Collaborating to build

When the team prepared their Scrum Board, they selected their first Tasks. The programmers will confirm the solution design and start coding. The analysts will start producing more detailed documentation. The testers will prepare their testing approach. This interplay of disciplines continues – collaborating and discussing – until all Tasks for all PBIs are completed.

Tracking progress continuously

As the team works, they make their individual progress clear by ensuring the Scrum Board always represents the actual work in progress at every moment of the day. At least once per day they will all stand together around the Scrum Board, for their Daily Scrum. If they are at all concerned about their progress, they will re-plan their approach to the remaining work.

Uncovering new work

As the Sprint progresses, the team will often find new work that they had not considered or expected during Sprint Planning. This is one of the main causes for a team being unable to complete a PBI in a single Sprint. For example, the team discovers that:

- A Task takes longer than anticipated.

- The PBI is more complicated and requires additional Tasks.

- A Bug has been found in something already developed.

- They are now dependent on work by another team or a specialist role.

Whenever a new Task is identified, it should be added to the Sprint Backlog and Scrum Board, with an estimate of how long the team think it will take. If existing work is blocked, for whatever reason, this should also be clearly marked.

This ensures that the whole team, the Product Owner, and other stakeholders get an accurate picture of the work remaining.

Technical practices in Scrum

While Scrum does not specify which technical practices to use, most teams adopt the following techniques from **Extreme Programming**, which also gave us the User Story (see page 48).

Test-driven development

In **test-driven development**, programmers, testers, and analysts collaborate to define how functionality will be tested. Once those unit tests are automated, programmers will keep coding up until the test is passed and then they stop. This improves quality and reduces the likelihood of adding unneeded functionality.

In acceptance test-driven development, the associated Acceptance Criteria are also automated. Finally, for behavior-driven development, interaction with the product is also automated (see Specification by example, in Chapter Four).

Continuous integration

To ensure the Delivery Team is working on the latest version, they should regularly merge their local copies into the shared code-base. This should take place at least once per day or even every few hours, and trigger a series of automated tests that confirm the integrity of existing functionality.

Refactoring

Test-driven principles promote the behavior of writing the least amount of code required to pass the tests. While this results in a product that is externally functional and fit for purpose, it can also be badly structured or not sufficiently commented. This can cause difficulties later and is one example of Technical Debt (page 117).

When programmers later revisit what they have built, they should consider improving it, making it simpler and more robust, without affecting its external, functional behavior. This is called **Refactoring**.

Pair programming

Many programmers prefer to work independently, sharing their work only when it is merged. While this enables them to focus, it limits the full team in knowing how the whole product functions.

In **pair programming**, two people work on the same Task side-by-side. One focuses on the technical detail, while the other continually reviews their deliverables while being mindful of other work coming up. To share the workload evenly, they should switch roles frequently.

Don't forget

Despite its name, the *pair programming* approach can be used successfully on any type of Task; i.e. not just *programming*.

Monitoring Task completion

For the team to know how well they are progressing through the Sprint, it is critical that all team members actively share their individual progress.

Reflecting progress on the Scrum Board

As members of the team take on a Task, they move the Task card to the In Progress column on the Scrum Board, so that everyone can see that the Task has been started. Most teams also stick an avatar onto the Task to show who it is assigned to. If they use a digital agile management tool, they will update the Task there too.

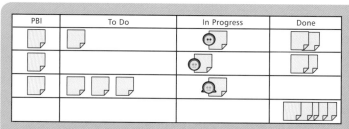

Typical Scrum Board, part way through a Sprint

Whenever they take a significant break, possibly lunch-time and certainly overnight, team members should ensure the Task card is still showing In Progress and update it with their estimate of the hours remaining to complete the Task.

When they have completed the Task, they should move it into the Done column, set the remaining hours to zero, and then look at the next possible Task for the same Product Backlog Item (PBI):

- If the next Task should be taken on by someone else, they should talk to them to let them know it is ready to start.

- If the next Task is dependent on someone else finishing their Task first, they should see if they can help them.

- If there are no more Tasks they can do for that PBI, they should look for the next most important PBI in the Sprint Backlog with a Task that they can work on.

- If there are no Tasks left that they could do, or there is not enough time left to start a new Task, they should see whether anyone else in the team needs help getting their Tasks completed.

Once all Tasks for a PBI are completed, the Task cards moved to the Done column, and the hours remaining set to zero, then the card for the PBI itself can also be moved across into the Done column. This makes it very clear that there are no remaining Tasks for that PBI, and it can be closed.

The Product Owner will often ask for a demonstration so that they can confirm and approve that the PBI can be closed (see Chapter Eight).

Estimate of remaining hours to complete

As a product development framework, Scrum is focused on how long it will take to complete work rather than how long it has taken so far. When the team updates a Task with their estimate of the hours remaining, they should not simply subtract the hours they have worked so far from the original estimate, instead they should re-estimate the work based on how much simpler or more complex they consider the work has become.

Sometimes the remaining hours are fewer than originally estimated, indicating that the work will be finished sooner. It is more likely, however, that the remaining hours will be higher, meaning the work will take longer. Knowing this as early as possible, even on the first Task on the first day, ensures that the team gets an early warning. Even small increases can often lead to significant delays, a knock-on impact to other PBIs, their Sprint goal, and even other teams.

On their first day, the team at Dante's discovered a significant amount of work. Joe, their Scrum Master, made a note to raise at their first Daily Scrum that 100 hours had been added to their total estimate to complete.

Record of actual hours done

While the focus for Scrum is the estimate to complete, many organizations also run some form of timesheet reporting. They will need to capture the number of hours spent on each PBI each day, as well as the estimate to complete.

While Scrum is not concerned with such issues, most digital agile management tools support team members recording hours done as well as hours remaining. The best tools will use this information to generate timesheets for each team member automatically.

Hot tip

Rather than leave it to the end of the Sprint, the Product Owner should review and approve whether a PBI is truly Done as soon as the team consider their work complete.

Beware

While timesheets may be important to your organization, in Scrum the only critical time-related information is *estimate to complete*.

Tracking progress

Team members share their progress by updating and moving their respective Task cards on the Scrum board. This is often summarized with a Sprint Burn-Down Chart as well.

The Burn-Down Chart is normally updated by hand as part of the team's physical Scrum Board. Where teams are able to update Tasks in a digital agile management tool, this automatically updates their digital Scrum Board and Sprint Burn-Down Chart.

The Sprint Burn-Down Chart

The Sprint Burn-Down Chart tracks units of work remaining towards a target of zero. Typically, this is based on the hours estimated to complete remaining Tasks each day in the Sprint.

Hot tip

Some teams choose to track a count of Tasks remaining, the number of Story points remaining, or even just a count of the Stories remaining.

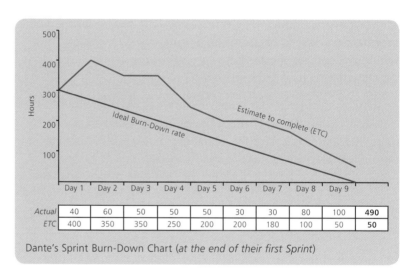

	Day 1	Day 2	Day 3	Day 4	Day 5	Day 6	Day 7	Day 8	Day 9	
Actual	40	60	50	50	50	30	30	80	100	**490**
ETC	400	350	350	250	200	200	180	100	50	**50**

Dante's Sprint Burn-Down Chart (*at the end of their first Sprint*)

The units (usually hours) are shown on the vertical y-axis, while elapsed time (each day of the Sprint) are shown on the horizontal x-axis.

Making your Sprint Burn-Down Chart

At the beginning of the Sprint, the total estimate is plotted on the y-axis. From this initial estimate, a straight line is drawn from that point to zero on the final day on which they could deliver. This line represents the ideal trend; that is, it assumes that if the team burns down the same average amount of work each day, they should have everything completed by the end of the Sprint.

In the example above, the red line represents where Dante's team plotted the work they forecast in Sprint Planning.

Tracking progress with the Sprint Burn-Down Chart

Each day, the remaining estimate to complete is plotted for that day, and joined with a line to the preceding day. If the team progresses well, the new points are plotted on or below the ideal trend line. If the team encounters problems, the new points are plotted above the ideal trend line. Staying above the line for too long indicates that the team is less likely to complete everything.

Dante's Sprint Burn-Down Chart shows how the team were tracking progress through their first Sprint.

Looking at this, we can see the actual work remaining each day jumped above the ideal trend line on the first day of the Sprint and stayed above it all the way to the end of the Sprint. The chart also shows us that the team ended the Sprint with 50 hours of work left to do. While we have not yet looked at their Scrum Board, this already suggests that they were unable to complete all the work they had planned – which probably means that at least one Product Backlog Item did not reach the Done state.

In terms of actual effort, the team invested 490 hours in this Sprint. That is just 10 hours under the 500 hours they calculated for their capacity in Sprint Planning (see page 96).

Their original estimate for the Sprint was just 300 hours, yet after 490 hours' effort they still had an estimate to complete of 50 hours left. What went wrong? Here are two things we can see from their Sprint Burn-Down Chart:

- On the first day of the Sprint, the team discovered 100 hours of additional Tasks – this suggests that they had not fully considered the work before planning it.

- Then on day three and day six they spent 50 hours and 30 hours of effort, but failed to reduce the estimate to complete – the equivalent of treading water – this suggests they had some challenges that blocked them.

Next, we will observe what happened at their Daily Scrums: how they tried to make sense of what was happening and what steps they tried in order to deal with it.

Replan at the Daily Scrum

Once the team has started to build the product, they continually monitor progress on their Scrum Board and Sprint Burn-Down Chart. Each day, they gather around their Scrum Board to consider their progress and make sense of whether they need to re-plan.

Teams that solely use a digital agile management tool will instead gather around a screen displaying their digital Scrum Board.

This daily gathering is known as the Daily Scrum event, and represents the fifth and final planning level (see Chapter Five).

Rules of the Daily Scrum

All team members are required to attend the Daily Scrum. To encourage attendance, it should be held in the same place at the same time – normally first thing in the morning.

To help the team stay focused, the Daily Scrum is time-boxed to just 15 minutes. While the team should share what's happening, this does not allow them time to get into detail – any Impediments raised are noted and the team moves on. Anyone with the knowledge or skills to discuss a potential solution waits until after the Daily Scrum to talk about it (taking it offline).

To maintain focus, most teams also adopt a format where each member takes turn in responding to three questions:

1 What have I completed – since we last met – that contributes to our Sprint goal?

2 What do I plan to complete next that contributes to our Sprint goal?

3 Do I see any real or potential Impediments that could block us from achieving our Sprint goal?

These questions help them describe their progress on Stories, Defects, and Tasks; focusing particularly on what is left to do.

What I have completed

Each team member shares what they have been able to complete – briefly at a high-level rather than hour-by-hour detail. The related cards should already have been moved on the Scrum Board, but if not they should update the Scrum Board as they talk.

What I plan to complete next

Next they share their high-level plan for the coming day. This enables the rest of the team to know about any upcoming work that could become ready for them. This is also the time to check that the estimate to complete is reducing sufficiently.

Any Impediments – real or potential

Finally, they share anything that could impede their work. This could range from their computer crashing, being blocked on a Task, or becoming unavailable (e.g. because of a doctor's appointment).

How the team responds to challenges

In looking at Dante's Sprint Burn-Down Chart (see page 108), we can tell that they were having issues from Day one. Let's observe what happened at some of their Daily Scrums:

- **Day two**: the team discussed the 100 hours of additional Tasks they had found, and felt that this was not a major problem – they had planned out only 300 hours of their 500 hour capacity, which meant they still had a buffer of 100 hours.

- **Day four**: in spite of 50 hours' effort on day three, their estimate to complete had not gone down – three of their Stories were blocked by Bugs that they did not know how to resolve – others team members offered to work with them.

- **Day seven**: after another 30 hours' effort on day six, they saw that they had again not reduced their estimate to complete – four of them had been unable to check in their work – the Scrum Master agreed to help them with that.

- **Day eight**: the team was happy that after 30 hours' effort, they had reduced the estimate to complete by 20 hours – one member lost time helping another team – now with two days remaining and 180 hours left, they agreed to work longer.

- **Day nine**: in their last Daily Scrum, they celebrated completing 80 hours' work the previous day, and reducing the estimate to complete to just 100 hours remaining – with only one day left in the Sprint, the team again committed to an extraordinary effort to get the work completed.

In the Sprint Review and Sprint Retrospective, we will find out what they achieved on that last day and what they have learned.

Too much work In Progress leads to context switching (see page 118); increasing the time to complete work, reducing throughput, and often resulting in the team not delivering their Sprint Backlog.

Swarming to complete work

When teams starts work on their Sprint Backlog, there is always a temptation for them to take on a separate area of work each. Starting as many Stories as possible might seem sensible, with the expectation that this will result in more work completed. However, teams that start Sprints like this are likely to end with several of the Stories they started on the first day still incomplete.

Stop Thrashing

Putting too much work In Progress reduces the ability of a team to be flexible, to pair on work or to cover for someone. Focus becomes divided, increasing the need to switch back and forth between different Stories and Tasks. This type of context switching is known as **Thrashing** and has been shown to increase stress levels and increase the time to complete work by up to 40%.

The team at Dante's had all started on separate Stories at the same time. When they encountered the problem of not being able to check anything in, they were all blocked at the same time. If they had been collaborating on the same work, they would have been able to recognize it as a common problem and resolve it together.

Start Swarming

Rather than Thrashing, it is better for teams to work together on their highest priority work, only starting something new when they have finished what they started first.

High-performing teams focus more on how to complete Stories to the Acceptance Criteria and Definition of Done. They can be more certain of completing their Product Increment. This is sometimes referred to as "*stop starting and start finishing*".

The benefits of **Swarming** include:

- Faster closure by designing, coding, testing and documenting to completion for each Story.

- Being able to resolve any Impediments immediately.

- Decreasing the likelihood of Bugs and Defects through pairing.

- Sharing knowledge and avoiding single points of failure.

- Completing high priority Stories first ensures that later Impediments only impact lower priority ones.

Key strategies for Swarming

- To learn how to Swarm, try it first on something small like a Spike, Defect, or Impediment.
- Get the whole team to work together on the same Story.
- Pair within Swarms to collaborate more closely.
- Check in more frequently to get a sense of progress.
- Update the estimate to complete more frequently to keep visibility of work remaining.
- Swarm as often as possible to build problem-solving skills.

How teams Swarm

Everyone should try to take a Task from the highest priority Story. Only look at Tasks for the second Story when any remaining Tasks for the first are dependent on others in progress.

While the whole team might work on just the first one or two Stories for the first couple of days, there will be a real sense of achievement when they can close the first Story by the middle of the first week. This acts to lift morale, boost productivity, and is a key step toward the team becoming high-performing.

When a Story is moved to the Done column, the Product Owner should check that the finished work meets the Acceptance Criteria and Definition of Done.

If the Product Owner cannot approve the Story as Done, it is rejected and should be moved back to the first column, and the team should add new Tasks to handle whatever is missing.

As that Story is likely to be higher in priority than any work that they then have in progress, the team needs to decide how to complete the missing work. How they do this will depend on how much time they have left in the current Sprint:

- Early in the Sprint: it may be safe to wait until they have finished the Task on which they are working – to then pick up one of the Tasks just added to the higher priority Story.

- Later in the Sprint: it would be better for them to pause anything they have in progress – so that they can focus on completing the Tasks just added to the higher priority Story.

Bugs, Defects and Incidents

As teams build, test, and document functionality, they will often detect something unwanted, incomplete, or broken in the product. This has to be captured and prioritized against other work, to be fixed at the appropriate time. Its priority will depend on the **Category**, **Severity**, and **Urgency**.

Category
The Category records when it was detected:

- **Bug**: detected while still being developed – that is, in the same Sprint.

- **Defect**: detected after being approved as Done – also known as Bugs that escaped the Sprint.

- **Incident**: detected after being released to market – also known as Bugs that escaped into the wild.

Severity
The Severity indicates the impact it has on use of the product:

- **Critical**: the whole product is non-functioning and unusable.

- **Major**: while some areas of the product are non-functioning, the rest of the product is still usable.

- **Moderate**: while the product exhibits some undesirable behavior, most of the functionality is usable.

- **Minor**: while the product exhibits some undesirable behavior, the product is functional enough to work around it.

- **Cosmetic**: while the outward appearance of the product is not quite right, the product is fully functional for normal use.

Urgency
The Urgency tells us how soon it should be resolved:

- **High**: must be resolved as soon as possible – immediately if already affecting customers.

- **Medium**: can wait to be resolved as part the next Release.

- **Low**: an irritant that can wait for a future Release or may safely be ignored.

Beware

While these are typical values for Category, Severity, and Urgency; these often vary by organization.

Triage

Whenever new Bugs, Defects, or Incidents are detected, they should be triaged. This involves:

1 Assess the Category, Severity, and Urgency

2 Check that it is not a duplicate and it can be reproduced

3 Prioritize to determine the next steps

How to prioritize in Triage

In prioritizing, the critical decision is whether it needs to be handled immediately or can be deferred.

- Treat a critical or major incident or a high Urgency Defect like a fire alarm, all work in progress stops until it is resolved.

- Treat a critical or major Defect as the next most important Product Backlog Item, to be resolved when someone is free.

- Treat a Bug like a new Task for the related Story, to be resolved in the same Sprint.

- Anything else should be added to the Product Backlog and prioritized later by the Product Owner like anything else.

A note about customer support and Incidents

Delivery Teams tend to be the third tier of product support. The first tier would be dedicated customer-facing roles who are able to resolve most Incidents directly with the customer. The second tier would be experts who help with training and configuration. By the third tier, most Incidents will already have been triaged.

Impact on Capacity and Velocity

Some organizations involve their Delivery Teams more directly in supporting the product they developed. This is intended to encourage a higher level of quality in the first instance.

However, as this type of unplanned work reduces capacity for planned work, there is a higher risk that the team will end their Sprints with work not completed. To allow for this, teams with an explicit responsibility to handle customer Incidents should plan their Sprint Backlog based on a reduced Capacity (see page 96).

Triage is an armed forces term for how they rapidly assess the injured – would they recover if they receive the right immediate intervention, recover by themselves, or likely not recover at all.

A Story cannot be closed while it has incomplete Tasks associated with it; this is why we treat a Bug like a Task for a Story.

Focusing on quality

Product Backlog Items (PBIs) focus mainly on defining the product's functionality, with behaviors and expected outcomes described in the Acceptance Criteria and specifications by example.

This emphasis on functionality needs to be balanced by paying attention to quality and technical excellence. The most common way teams reinforce their commitment to these non-functional principles is to include them in their Definition of Done.

Tracking quality

Teams track their progress throughout the Sprint on their Scrum Board and Sprint Burn-Down Chart (see page 108). This needs to be balanced by tracking key non-functional metrics too.

The following metrics have been found useful in summarizing and focusing on how product quality is trending:

- **Automated test coverage**: measures the proportion of Features in the product covered by automated tests – to avoid regression testing becoming a bottle-neck in product development, all common testing should be automated. As functionality is added to the product, the Definition of Done should ensure that any new tests are also automated.

- **Defect removal efficiency**: measures the proportion of Defects detected and resolved before the product is released to market, against the number that escape into the wild – the higher the proportion, the better the attention to quality.

- **Aged Defect analysis**: measures how long Defects of each Severity and Urgency have been in the product – borrowed from the accountancy concept of aged debt analysis, this highlights the number of Defects that are up to 30 days old, 30-60 days, 60-90 days, and over 90 days – focusing on quality should see the numbers shift into shorter periods.

- **Defect origins**: measures a count of Defects arising from each source – how the product was defined, how the solution was designed, how the functionality was coded, how a Bug was fixed, or how the product was deployed.

When reading these metrics it is better to look at trends rather than individual numbers – whether the metric is steady, improving or getting worse.

Zero Defects

A commitment to quality and technical excellence is often reflected in a policy of **Zero Defects**. This does not mean that there will never be Bugs. On the contrary, it is expected and preferred that a team will detect Bugs and resolve them during a Sprint. That is one of the key benefits of cross-functional teams with all disciplines working side-by-side.

A policy of Zero Defects should mean that no Bugs are allowed to escape a Sprint to become Defects, let alone escape into the wild to become Incidents. Any Bugs unresolved at the end of a Sprint will mean the associated Story should not be closed, but rather carried over into the following Sprint – unless the Product Owner deems the Story to be of such little value that it can be dropped.

Technical Debt

Product Owners want to deliver as much Business Value to their customers as possible. The value produced as a proportion of the effort involved can be derived as a rough measure for return on investment. However, this assumes that the value of the product increases as work is carried out on it.

Unfortunately, teams are often driven to deliver more than they can reliably complete, which often results in them not developing the functionality in the most well-structured, cleanest, or robust way. Corners get cut. Some Acceptance Criteria might even be re-negotiated as non-mandatory.

The Product Owner could even choose to close a Story with an unresolved Bug, so long as that Bug is first converted into a Defect. Whenever the Product Owner accepts this, they are effectively agreeing to put some work off until a later date. This acts as a negative counterbalance to the value being added – hence the metaphor of **Technical Debt**.

Releasing product updates to market with known Technical Debt begins to erode the value of the product. Too much Technical Debt will eventually start to degrade the customer experience and make it easier for them to decide to switch to a competitor's product.

Just as organizations can adopt a policy of Zero Defects, so too should they consider proactively paying down Technical Debt – through techniques like refactoring (see page 105), for example.

Handling interruptions

As we saw in Chapter Two, one of the core values of Scrum is *Focus*. In order for the team to deliver on their Sprint Backlog, it is important that they can focus on their work. However, teams are faced with interruptions as an everyday occurrence.

There are many reasons for interruptions: urgent customer issues, company meetings, requests for help, management walkabouts, and so forth. It is common to get an invitation or request at short notice, and in the moment decide that what is being asked sounds important, and to then just do it.

For example, in their eighth Daily Scrum, we learned that the team at Dante's lost one of their developers for a day, to help resolve a problem elsewhere.

The problems of context switching

People often don't realize the full impact of interrupting and taking one or more team members off their Sprint Backlog. In particular, when working on a complex Task, the cost of context switching can easily add a further 30 minutes to time lost due to the interruption. It takes a little while to be able to safely down tools without leaving too many loose ends. After the interruption has concluded, it then takes time to get back into the right mindset to tackle complex product development again.

Often these types of interruptions are unavoidable, and teams need a plan for how to recognize interruptions, confirm if they are critical (urgent and important), and manage them appropriately. Unchecked, interruptions will eventually stop the team delivering their whole Sprint Backlog.

The following techniques can help handle interruptions:

Follow the Scrum guidelines

Scrum requires teams to work transparently, and to inspect and adapt. Whenever someone recognizes that they have been interrupted for something not in their Sprint Backlog, they should log it. The most common approach for this is for the affected team member to write the interruption and amount of time lost on a sticky-note and then attach it to their Scrum Board at the Daily Scrum, where they can share with the team what happened. The team should add these up to explain in their Sprint Review where they had lost any of their capacity. They should also review them in their Sprint Retrospective to identify the root causes.

Negotiate the interruption

When the team realizes that they are being asked to do something that will interrupt them, before they carry it out they should show the requestor their Scrum Board and suggest they talk to the Product Owner to negotiate which planned Task should not be done, to free up time for their request.

This requires a degree of confidence that not every team member will have. The Scrum Master could always step up and act as gate keeper for the team. This is one of the reasons it is useful for the Scrum Master to sit with the team (see Chapter Two).

Adjust Capacity

Teams should make an allowance for general administration and planned non-team commitments when calculating their Capacity for Sprint Planning (see Chapter Six).

Interruptions

When working in an environment where interruptions are common, the team should consider one member triaging requests for their time. This should be the Scrum Master or Product Owner, even though it is unlikely they will be able to action it.

Responsibility for triaging requests for unplanned work should be rotated or shared by the team each Sprint.

Similar to triaging Bugs, Defects, and Incidents (see page 115), the team should consider a request's importance, urgency, and likely impact. Low impact requests can usually be absorbed into time allowed for general administration. High impact requests that are truly critical (that is, urgent and important) would be done, and where possible by the person doing the triage.

When following this approach, Capacity for the team should be reduced sufficiently. It is unlikely that a team member will want to triage for more than a Sprint at a time, so it is wise for teams to rotate this responsibility.

Accept reality and downgrade Velocity

Where the degree of interruption consistently acts to stop teams delivering their full Sprint Backlog, they could consider reducing their target Velocity (see Chapter Six) until they reach the level they can reliably deliver. While this is transparent, it does nothing to mitigate the root causes. Left unchecked, such teams will likely become demoralized and will be likely to experience productivity that continues to slip even lower.

It is better to invest time in resolving root causes than to accept high levels of interruptions, as these are typically caused by unseen Impediments.

Risks and Impediments

While the Delivery Team focuses on delivering their Sprint Backlog, there will always be unforeseen problems that can block their work. These are loosely termed an **Impediment**.

Impediments could be potential (i.e. Risks) or actual (i.e. already occurred). Teams should treat Dependencies (other work that has to be completed first) and Assumptions (operating conditions that must stay true) as potential Impediments too. The abbreviation RIDA is often used to refer generically to Risks, Impediments, Dependencies, and Assumptions.

As soon as an actual or potential Impediment is identified, the team should actively manage it. They need to capture it, assess it, agree how to respond, and continue to monitor it until it has passed. The aim of Risk management is to stop it from becoming an Impediment or to minimize its impact should that occur.

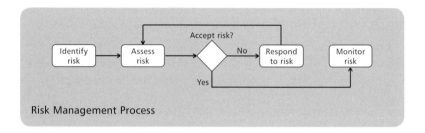

Risk Management Process

Identifying Risks and Impediments

Whoever identified it should capture a short description with where and when it was found. This is typically on a sticky-note or index card, attached to their Scrum Board or a separate shared Risk Board (see page 132), to be visible at all times.

RIDA	Type: Risk | Impediment | Dependency | Assumption	
Date raised: / /	Description and impact:	Impact date: / /
Date closed: / /		
Owned by:	Action:	Resolved | Mitigated | Accepted
Impact: 1 | 2 | 3 | 4 | 5		Likelihood: 1 | 2 | 3 | 4 | 5

Assessing Risks and Impediments

The team should next assess the potential impact and likelihood, along with the date by which it might become critical. Assessment is typically on a 1-5 scale. For likelihood this represents a range from *unlikely* through to *it has already occurred*. For impact, this ranges from *minimal* to *severe*. A Risk score should then be calculated by multiplying the assessments for impact and likelihood. Any Risk score in the range 1-6 would be low risk, 7-14 medium, and 15 or above would be considered high risk.

For example: in their first Sprint, the likelihood that the team at Dante's will underestimate the work required is high, but the impact would be low (as they have time to make up for it). Later on, when they become more confident in sizing their work, the likelihood should become low, but as they near the end of the Release, the impact of getting that wrong would be higher.

Responding to Risks and Impediments

When the team have assessed the impact, they should decide what actions to take and who owns the responsibility for that. Responses typically include Resolution, Mitigation, or Acceptance. In mitigating a Risk or Impediment, the team will take steps to reduce its impact or likelihood. In resolving it, the team will fix or remove the underlying problem. In accepting it, the team has agreed that they can live with the implications.

For anything that is high impact and highly likely or already happened, the team should take action immediately. If the team does not have the capacity or capability to resolve it, the Scrum Master would normally look for other parties who can.

Monitoring Risks and Impediments

The ongoing status of any Risks, Impediments, Dependencies, or Assumptions should be tracked and reviewed regularly. Teams could consider them at the end of their Daily Scrum or at a Scrum of Scrums (see Chapter Ten). As with the interruptions (see page 118), include them in the Sprint Review and Sprint Retrospective.

The risk score should be regularly re-assessed – if the likelihood or impact increases or decreases, this should trigger a re-evaluation. Finally, it can be closed off when the Risk score becomes very low or it has been resolved, becomes irrelevant, or has simply gone away.

Summary

- Focus on the minimum required to complete Product Backlog Items (PBIs) with test-driven development – an Extreme Programming (XP) practice where unit tests are defined and automated, then development continues until the tests pass.

- Keep intrinsic quality high and Technical Debt low by allowing time for refactoring – an XP practice where the product's internal quality is improved without changing its external functional behavior.

- Get immediate feedback on the integrity of functionality with continuous integration – an XP practice where newly checked-in code is automatically built, integrated, and tested.

- Improve team resilience and knowledge-sharing through pair programming – an XP practice where two team members jointly work on Tasks from the Sprint Backlog together.

- Improve the flow of priority work by Swarming – where team members work together to complete the highest priority PBIs before starting anything else.

- Keep the Scrum Board and agile management tool updated at all times – moving cards to the appropriate state, flagging items as blocked, and updating estimates to complete.

- When any new work is uncovered, add it to the Sprint Backlog – unless it is significant and not required to get the PBI done, in which case add it to the Product Backlog.

- The progress of the team overall should be tracked using a Sprint Burn-Down Chart, as this helps them to forecast when they can complete their Sprint Backlog.

- Once per day, at the Daily Scrum, the team gather for 15 minutes by their Scrum Board to review progress, consider any Impediments, and re-plan the remaining work if needed.

- Focus on quality by resolving Bugs as soon as they arise, and giving Defects and Incidents the appropriate priority.

- Maintain the focus of the team by keeping interruptions and Impediments to a minimum, or resolving them promptly when they do occur.

8 Delivering the Product Increment

Having built the next Product Increment, the team needs to review and deploy it. This chapter looks at integration, deployment, and stakeholder review.

The Product Increment

For the adoption of Scrum to be successful as a feedback-driven product development framework, the team must deliver working software each and every Sprint. That is, all the Product Backlog Items (PBIs) that the team completes in a Sprint, must be agreed as meeting the Acceptance Criteria and Definition of Done, be fully integrated, and be fit to release to the customer.

Recalling the origins of Scrum as an approach to iterative design and incremental development, the team's work from a Sprint is combined with the work from all previous Sprints to become the next Product Increment. This is repeated each Sprint, with the team iteratively building new increments of the product.

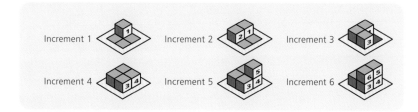

Potentially Shippable Increment

The Product Owner decides whether to release a Product Increment to market, or to wait for more functionality to be added. For this reason, the Product Increment is often referred to as a Potentially Shippable Increment (or PSI).

The PBIs the team selected will be a combination of new Features, modifications to existing functionality, and improvements to quality. The product progressively increases in value with each successive increment. The Product Owner will often choose to wait for a minimum amount of value to be added to their product before releasing it to market. This may take more than one Sprint.

All work intended to be potentially shippable should be fully integrated by the end of the Sprint. This means that integration is one of the tasks required for each PBI, so is typically included in the Definition of Done. The benefits of doing this include:

- Reduced risk, by not leaving critical work undone until later.

- Improved transparency, giving confidence it is really Done.

- Increased throughput, by reducing work in progress.

Don't forget

The *potential* of *Potentially Shippable* indicates only that the Product Increment may be released if required, not that the quality or fitness is uncertain.

The challenge of dependencies

With more complex products, however, the team will often be dependent on the work of other teams or organizations. While new Features might be capable of basic functionality, without the dependent work they cannot deliver the intended value.

In such situations, the Product Owner is forced to choose between waiting for dependent work to be completed, or removing the new functionality which has incomplete dependencies. Although it goes against the spirit of Scrum, they will typically choose to wait.

To minimize the risk of this, it is critical to identify and manage any dependencies as early as possible. It is best to start well before the team is likely to work on the affected PBIs, such as during the Discovery workshops (see Chapter Three).

The need for the Release cycle

Planning and monitoring work at the Release level allows us to better integrate the work of several Sprints with the work of other teams or organizations (see Chapter Five).

While the Release cycle is not formally recognized as part of Scrum, due to constraints such as these, most organizations would not be able to operate without it.

Stabilizing or hardening Sprints

Waiting for other work to be completed is frustrating for the teams involved, and is dysfunctional according to Scrum. However, this is a common occurrence. To cope with this, most teams will reserve the last Sprint of a Release for stabilizing – also known as hardening – the Product Increment.

This typically means that the team stops developing new functionality, and focuses instead on proving that the integrated functionality operates correctly. While the balance of work changes, this still requires all the disciplines to collaborate closely, testing to verify, coding to fix, and documenting for release.

In complex environments with many inter-dependencies, this can lead to an extended stabilization that lasts for several Sprints. This highlights significant organizational constraints and Impediments. Every effort should be taken to find ways of integrating and testing earlier to mitigate, reduce, or avoid this altogether. The next topic explores ways of achieving this.

Continuous path to market

In Chapter Seven we learned about continuous integration. To overcome the need for stabilization and be able to release to market more frequently, everything needs to be continuous.

Continuous integration for Release readiness

As team members check in their work, this should trigger a rebuild of the product and run a series of automated tests. In order to support Release readiness, as far as possible these tests should verify that the Product Increment will integrate correctly with all dependent Features and services.

If the build breaks or any of the critical tests fail, the merge should be reversed and the team should be prompted to resolve it immediately. This ensures that the product is always in a functioning state, and means that potential problems are trapped and resolved as early as possible.

Continuous deployment

Scrum requires that working software should be potentially releasable at the end of each and every Sprint. For organizations working in particularly competitive or demanding markets, however, this may not be frequent enough.

In order to radically reduce their lead-time, such organizations typically invest in extending the continuous integration approach, so that changes can be deployed as soon as they have been integrated and verified. This puts new functionality into customers' hands and provides the possibility for very short feedback loops.

Continuous deployment requires an investment in infrastructure to automate all the steps through integration, verification, and release. It is therefore largely applicable only to *software as a service* products or those that are capable of being updated *over the air* (i.e. through mobile or Wi-Fi networks).

Continuous delivery

Organizations with products that require manual intervention to be distributed or installed cannot truly support continuous deployment. However, they can get close to these principles.

Continuous delivery requires operations staff capable of the fast turn-around of critical manual steps. For example, being able to rapidly deploy products that have passed automated integration and verification testing.

The rise of DevOps

While Scrum provides an effective framework for product development, as organizations adapt to deploying their products more frequently, they encounter a greater impact on the operational side of their business.

To be really successful in getting their product into the hands of customers, to generate feedback or revenue, organizations need to ensure as smooth a path as possible from their development to their operational environments and teams.

This focus on bridging the perceived gap between *Development* and *Operations* led to the evolving field of **DevOps**.

The continuous involvement of operational teams

A key requirement for DevOps is that operational teams are continuously engaged with the Delivery Team throughout the product development process.

Operational teams include not just those who deploy, configure, and operate the product, but also those who sell it, who support customers, and who invoice for its ongoing operation.

These groups need to be involved right from the start when the Product Vision is established. It is also strongly recommended that they form part of the Discovery Team (see Chapter Three).

Balancing functional and non-functional needs

The Product Owner is rightfully very focused on what the customer needs, but this has to be balanced with what the organization itself needs. While customers' needs are generally regarded as functional in nature, the organization's operational needs are often regarded as Non-Functional Requirements or qualities of service (see Chapter Four). Critical qualities of service should be captured in the Definition of Done, as this ensures they are attended to for each and every Product Backlog Item.

As the product itself evolves and matures, it will often need work to address changing requirements around qualities of service. This means that the Product Backlog should also reflect a balance of non-functional work as well (see Chapter Five). For example, this could cover concerns such as performance improvements, changes to the way the product is deployed to market, and enhancements in security protocols.

Reviewing the team's work

Now that they have finished their Sprint, the team need to show their progress to their stakeholders. This enables them to get feedback to guide what they plan for the next Sprint. The Sprint Review should be around two hours for a two-week Sprint.

Preparing for the Sprint Review

Thinking about the Sprint Review should start as early as Sprint Planning, or even Backlog Refinement. The team should consider how they will demonstrate that their work meets the Acceptance Criteria and Definition of Done. This will often encourage them to design test scenarios that would better resonate with stakeholders as well as driving them to build with that in mind.

Facilitating a successful Review

The team should decide who will tell the Story of their Sprint and who will demonstrate the product. This is a great opportunity to develop public speaking confidence, as well as pride in their work.

1. Recap the purpose of the Sprint Review, remind everyone of the time limit, and encourage constructive feedback

2. Set the scene, explain the team's goal for that Sprint, and set the theme for the demonstrations that are to follow

3. Compare the work they completed with what they forecast in Sprint Planning, and highlight any events that had an impact on their planned Capacity

4. Then, for each item completed in that Sprint:

   - Explain what scenarios it was intended to cover

   - Demonstrate how it meets those scenarios

   - Collect any concerns or ideas for additional work

5. Show the team's overall progress towards being ready for the Release (the Release Burn-Up Chart)

6. Close by recapping on key feedback and thank people for their time and contribution

Make it worth while attending

The most valuable aspect of the Sprint Review is getting timely feedback from stakeholders. Ensure their attendance in future Sprints by giving them a compelling and memorable experience.

Take the time to tell a story, use a series of scenarios involving real-world examples of people, places, and activities. This will make the experience far more vivid for stakeholders. If possible, have stakeholders interact with the product. They will be far more likely to pay attention and to provide valuable feedback.

While you would not do this every Sprint, consider a company-wide showcase. This would not only reach far more stakeholders, it would also be good promotion for the work the team is doing.

Be honest about the team's progress – success and failure

In their first Sprint, the team at Dante's failed to complete three Product Backlog Items they had selected. The first had turned out to be far more complex than expected. The second had been blocked waiting for another team to complete dependent work. The last had been blocked because of a Bug they could not fix.

The Product Owner considered closing the third one, converting its Bug into a Defect, but the team felt uncomfortable with that.

They also had several interruptions that reduced their Capacity. Teams can find it hard to recall every time they were interrupted during the Sprint, so it is useful to record these as they occur.

Capture feedback into the Product Backlog

Any significant feedback from stakeholders should be captured into the Product Backlog, either as additional Acceptance Criteria or notes for existing PBIs, or more often as new PBIs that build on the work just demonstrated. These new PBIs would be refined and prioritized just as any others would be.

With any work they were unable to complete, they should provide a brief explanation and indicate how much work might be left. This will guide stakeholders in their feedback with what to:

- Treat as priority for the next Sprint

- Review and re-assess in the next Backlog Refinement

- Agree as low value and no longer worth the effort required

The Sprint Review is a great opportunity to gather feedback and to engage with stakeholders. Do not treat it purely as a time for demo and sign-off.

done, Done, DONE

By now, our team at Dante's has completed their first Sprint, their stakeholders have reviewed the work the Product Owner agreed was Done, and the Product Increment is ready to release. With only four Stories completed, however, the Product Owner decides to wait for some full Features to be completed before releasing.

As they work through the next few Sprints – adding functionality into each successive Product Increment – they realize that more is required to get their work integrated and ready for release.

Anything that stops the team from releasing every Sprint should be treated as an Impediment, and the team should actively work to resolve it until they can meet this core principle of Scrum.

Multi-level Definition of Done

Organizations may take some time to achieve this, and some constraints may mean this is never fully realized. However, the effects of this can be mitigated by using a multi-level Definition of Done. This defines progressively how the team determine that a Story is Done, that the full Feature is complete, and finally that Release can be shipped. Hence the term *done, Done, DONE*.

- **Story Definition of Done**: in Chapter Six, we learned that quality of service (Non-Functional) Requirements apply to all work – to be captured in a general Story Definition of Done that supplements the Acceptance Criteria for each Story.

- **Feature Definition of Done**: for complex Features, it may take a few Sprints to complete all the Stories – rather than writing and rewriting deliverables like training and documentation for each Story, these should be in a Feature Definition of Done.

- **Release Definition of Done**: organizations in heavily-regulated markets often have an additional overhead to releasing their products – such as third-party testing or complex hand-overs – these should be part of a Release Definition of Done which applies to all work when it has been completed.

While a multi-level Definition of Done does help the team work around such constraints, it exposes Organizational Impediments that should be actively managed to mitigate and resolve so that the team can release more frequently.

Tracking release progress

The **Release Burn-Up Chart** tracks the work from each Sprint during the Release on the horizontal x-axis, that incrementally contributes toward the target scope on the vertical y-axis.

Making a Release Burn-Up Chart

After Release Planning, the agreed scope is marked in Story points on the y-axis and a horizontal target line is drawn across.

An expected Velocity line is drawn from the chart's zero point up to meet the target scope by the final Sprint. If the team burns up at this rate, this shows they will deliver the agreed scope on time.

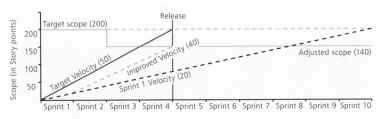

Dante's Release Burn-Up Chart

Tracking progress with the Release Burn-Up Chart

For each Sprint Review, the number of Story points completed in that Sprint is plotted. A new Velocity is calculated – based on the last three Sprints – and a line drawn from there to meet the scope. This indicates when the team might complete all the work.

- When progress is good, the lines meet the scope sooner – the product could be released earlier or scope could be added.

- When progress is slow, the line will reach the scope later – either scope should be dropped or the Release delayed.

As we can see from Dante's chart above, after their first Sprint they would have needed six additional Sprints to complete their scope. This is fairly typical of a new team. Although their Velocity will improve, they also chose to cut their scope to release in time.

Any change in scope is shown by re-plotting the target scope, as a step up or down – for example, see Sprint 3 above. Decreasing scope, by stepping the target scope down, means the forecast Velocity line will reach it sooner so that it can be released earlier. Increasing scope means the Release would be delayed.

Beware

Delay committing to additional scope until the last responsible moment, especially when tracking a high number of Risks and Dependencies.

Retiring Risk early

A single team working on a product has relatively little to track in terms of Risks, Impediments, Dependencies, and Assumptions (RIDAs). They would post any RIDAs on their Scrum Board and review them in their Daily Scrum and Sprint Retrospective.

Teams working on complex products and with dependencies on other teams will benefit from managing their RIDAs collectively.

The Risk Board

As with the Discovery Board (see Chapter Four) and the Scrum Board (see Chapters Six and Seven), the Risk Board is organized into columns that reflect the states that a RIDA can move through.

Don't forget

The Risk Board may also be known as a *RIDA, ROAM* or NORMA Board after the acronyms for types of risk or the states it can go through.

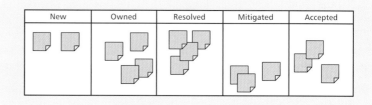

Any RIDA starts as new, until it is assessed and owned. The owner is then responsible for any corrective action and for monitoring the RIDA until it is Resolved, Mitigated, or Accepted. This reflects the Risk management process outlined in the preceding chapter (see page 120).

The RIDA radar

An alternative layout to tracking RIDAs by state, is instead to arrange them in columns according the Sprint in which they will cause problems if not resolved.

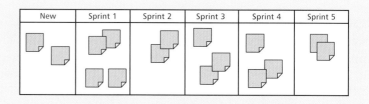

This visualization technique highlights the timeliness of attending to each RIDA, and encourages teams to focus more on those whose impact is more imminent.

At the end of each Sprint, any Risks or Dependencies that blocked work should be converted into Impediments. This means they will be treated with a higher priority. Any Risks or Dependencies whose time has passed and which have not blocked any work are marked as either Accepted or Resolved.

Monitoring overall risk with the Risk Burn-Down

As well as managing and tracking individual RIDAs, teams working on complex products should consider using the Risk Burn-Down Chart to visualize overall risk throughout the Release.

When the team discovers a RIDA, whether in Release Planning (see Chapter Five) or at any point after, they assess the potential impact and likelihood to calculate a Risk score (see Chapter Seven).

The Risk Burn-Down shows the level of overall risk (total Risk score) on the vertical y-axis, and elapsed time (each Sprint in the Release) on the horizontal x-axis.

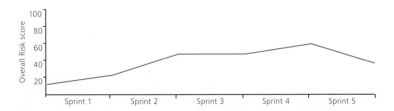

Tracking progress on the Risk Burn-Down Chart

After Release Planning, the total Risk score is marked on the y-axis. After each Sprint Planning, the total Risk score for all open risks is plotted against that Sprint and joined up with a line.

As the team manages RIDAs towards being Resolved, Mitigated, or Accepted, the associated Risk score will reduce (e.g. because the likelihood or impact has reduced). This should result in the line progressively sloping down to the right. As new RIDAs are discovered, there will be a corresponding jump in overall risk, which will be revealed by the line sloping up again.

The Risk Burn-Down Chart for the Dante's team shows that overall risk was not decreasing noticeably after the first two Sprints. When this happens, the team should explore the reasons in their next Sprint Retrospective (see Chapter Nine).

Summary

- The Sprint ends with a Sprint Review, in which the team and the stakeholders review the Product Increment, assess overall progress, and update the Product Backlog with any additional work agreed.

- Sprint Reviews are time-boxed to two hours for a typical two-week Sprint – pro-rata lower or higher for shorter or longer Sprint durations.

- The Product Increment is also known as Potentially Shippable Increment, as the Product Owner may delay release to combine several Product Increments.

- Ideally a team releases Product Increments every Sprint, but when they do not, it helps to distinguish what work is required to orchestrate and prepare the whole release – this has given rise to the multi-level Definition of Done.

- Where a team is waiting to combine several Product Increments, they should track their progress to completing the target scope through the Release Burn-Up Chart.

- When the Product Owner does decide to release a Product Increment, then a continuous deployment approach automates the Release process – any changes can be promoted to the production environment without further intervention.

- Where human intervention is required, a continuous delivery approach would mean someone would be available to support the team by promoting the product into the right environment.

- Following a DevOps approach would streamline the path to Release even better – this bridges the perceived gap between development and operations, and ensures that the product is designed with operational needs in mind as well.

- Just as teams manage their daily work on their Scrum Board, they should also actively manage their outstanding risks – if they are working with other teams, this could even be on a separate Risk Board that they review at the Scrum of Scrums.

- Teams should also actively monitor their exposure to risk via the Risk Burn-Down, which shows overall risk levels over time.

9 Continual improvement in Scrum

This chapter explores how the Scrum Master coaches the development of high-performing teams and guides organizations – from problem-solving, continual improvement, and transformation, to becoming a learning organization.

Looking back to go forward

Congratulations! By now, you have brought together your first Scrum Team and guided them through defining and delivering their first Product Increment. They have just presented this to their stakeholders and listened to feedback about what comes next.

As a feedback-driven framework for product development, Scrum is built on learning teams who make time to inspect and adapt. Before they start to prepare for their next Sprint, the team should take a moment to reflect on how effective they have been.

Why we hold a Retrospective every Sprint

As they close out a plan-driven project, the Project Manager holds a *post-mortem* – looking back to see what lessons may be learned. Any insights may be useful, but they are too late for that project, and by then people have often forgotten many of the challenges.

In Scrum, the Scrum Master facilitates a Sprint Retrospective each and every Sprint. Memories are still fresh, and changes can be made in the very next Sprint. Run well, this will also foster a sense of joint ownership and self-organization:

- **Improving morale**: teams should consider how they worked together, to highlight and deal with any misaligned behavior.

- **Improving effectiveness**: teams should explore how effective they were, to identify any activities that could be done better.

- **Action-oriented**: teams should agree SMART actions and add them to their Backlog, to avoid the same challenges again.

- **High performance**: every team should look for opportunities to continually improve towards high performance.

- **Organizational change**: teams should escalate any Impediments they have not been able to resolve themselves, so that they can request any additional support needed to resolve whatever has been blocking them.

The team at Dante's

As we have followed the Dante's team through their first Sprint, we encountered a number of Impediments, which they should consider in their Sprint Retrospective.

We will look at those in detail as we consider these five perspectives of the Retrospective.

Beware

Do not wait until all development has been completed before conducting a post-mortem or lessons learned session.

The Sprint Retrospective

The Sprint Retrospective is facilitated by the Scrum Master for the team to discuss the Sprint that has just ended, to celebrate what went well, and agree what could be done better. While the Sprint Review looks at what the team built, the Sprint Retrospective looks at how they went about building it.

When to run the Retrospective
The Sprint Retrospective should be the last activity at the end of a Sprint. Allow roughly 90 minutes for a two-week Sprint.

Who to invite
The Retrospective should involve the whole Scrum Team, including the Product Owner, the Delivery Team, and the Scrum Master.

Retrospectives need a safe space
Considering that the team may need to deal with issues relating to their morale or the behavior of an individual, the Retrospective is normally held in a room that is closed off from other people.

Key steps for a Retrospective
The Scrum Master facilitates the following Retrospective steps:

1 Set the stage, remind everyone what the Retrospective is for, and check how ready everyone is to contribute

2 Build the team's energy levels and sense of safety

3 Explore what happened in the Sprint to identify successes, problems and opportunities

4 Look for patterns and see what insights the team has

5 Analyze the main points together to agree on root causes

6 Choose actions that the team can take and for what might need escalating

Teams typically use structured activities such as games, which suspend normal rules and help create an alternate reality in which people can contribute. Hundreds of games have been developed for Retrospectives, some of which are covered in this chapter.

Hot tip

Teams should hold their Retrospective on the same day as their Sprint Review. This helps them mentally close down the Sprint before focusing on the next one.

Setting the stage

The Scrum Master sets the stage with a warm welcome, thanking team members for making the time to attend. After clarifying the purpose of the Retrospective they should get everyone to speak.

The team needs to feel safe enough to talk openly about anything effecting their morale or performance.

The Prime Directive

To help remind everyone why we hold a Retrospective, the Prime Directive is a foundational ground rule for creating a safe space:

> *"In considering what happened during the last Sprint, we all acknowledge that everyone did the best job they could: given what they knew at the time, their skills and abilities, the resources available, and the situation at hand."*

The Safety Check

Having set the context and reminded people that they should feel safe, a great technique to gauge the team's readiness to contribute is an exercise known as the **Safety Check**:

1 Give sticky-notes and marker pens to the whole team

2 Everyone writes a number to indicate how safe they feel

- [**5**] Willing and able to speak freely on everything
- [**4**] Willing to talk about almost anything
- [**3**] Will contribute, but not on difficult subjects
- [**2**] Will listen, but will be unlikely to contribute
- [**1**] Unable or unwilling to speak freely

3 Collect the sticky-notes anonymously – in a hat or a box

4 Draw a horizontal line on a whiteboard, split into five sections, numbered 1 to 5; then place each sticky-note on the line to form a growing column for each number

5 Review the spread of numbers and assess what this means for the team's readiness to contribute

The spread of numbers will help the team consider what to do next in their Retrospective:

- When the numbers are mostly high, this means the team are ready to deal with any subject and should move on to the next stage – looking at what happened during the Sprint.

- When the numbers are mostly middle range, the Scrum Master should offer to watch out for any sensitive subjects so they can step in if they sense anyone becoming uncomfortable – if the team agrees, they could still move on to the next stage.

- On the other hand, when the numbers are mostly low, it would be safer to adapt the agenda and focus instead on improving team morale and safety – perhaps using one of the games on pages 140-141. This would still be regarded as investing in a team improvement, as better morale would contribute to higher performance in the upcoming Sprint.

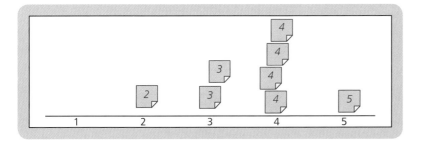

The team at Dante's ran the Safety Check for their first Sprint Retrospective, and it was no surprise that their numbers were quite low. They used a safety-building game before moving on.

An alternative to numbers for the Safety Check
Instead of using numbers, the team could write the first letter for whichever of the following personas best represents how they feel:

- **Explorer**: keen to contribute and learn, nothing is off-limits.

- **Shopper**: will observe and be happy if they get one new idea.

- **Vacationer**: interest is low, but welcome the break from work.

- **Prisoner**: there against their will, would rather be doing something they consider more productive.

Get the team in the mood

When the team's energy levels or safety feels low, it can help to run a short activity to boost morale and lift their energy. As soon as it feels like things are improving, either rerun the Safety Check or move straight on to the next stage. Here are four examples:

Candy Love
This exercise gets people talking about work as well as their life outside work. Pour a pack of colorful candy into a bowl, then take turns picking one and sharing something based on the color:

- **Red**: One great thing about the job or the work

- **Orange**: A favorite food or drink

- **Yellow**: A life goal or significant planned event

- **Green**: A book or a film that left a lasting impression

- **Blue**: One thing that causes stress

- **Purple**: A favorite way to overcome stress

Untangle Yourselves
In this exercise, participants stand in a circle – with their right hand they grab someone's left hand, with their left hand they grab someone else's right hand – but not their immediate neighbors. Now they have to untangle themselves – without letting go – moving under or over each other's hands to form a circle.

They should try this first without speaking, so they have to use gesture and facial expressions to communicate – however, allow the laughter that comes as they progressively untangle themselves.

Mob Rock-Paper-Scissors
For this exercise, participants form pairs – if there is anyone spare, they become someone else's supporter. On the count of three, each participant forms the shape of a rock, a piece of paper, or a pair of scissors with one hand. Rock beats scissors, scissors beats paper, and paper beats rock. Whoever wins – after the best of three – finds another winner ready for the next round, while whoever loses becomes their loud and vocal supporter.

After three rounds there should be one winner, at which point everyone loudly cheers for them. Teams often have so much fun with this, they run it more than once.

While these exercises are designed for Retrospectives, they can help in any situation where the team's mood or energy levels need lifting.

Mood Lines

When participants are struggling to talk about how they feel, another useful technique is Mood Lines:

1 Draw a short upright line on the left-hand side of a whiteboard, mark it with a positive sign at the top and a negative sign at the bottom – or a happy and sad face

2 Draw a horizontal line from the center of that first line right across the middle of the board, then mark off points along the horizontal line for each day in the Sprint

3 Each participant takes turns to come to the board with a whiteboard marker pen, and plot a line from the start to the end of the Sprint that reflects how positive or negative they felt each day during the Sprint. As their line moves up or down, the participant should share what was happening on that day – the Scrum Master might choose to capture a high or low point on a sticky-note and place it next to the corresponding peak or trough on the board

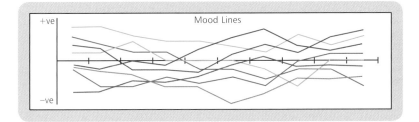

When the team at Dante's played this game, their mood lines looked like the diagram above. The board was filled with lines that crisscrossed, as each participant had a different experience or recollection. This is normal. We can see that team members felt better or worse at different times. Some were unhappy when work was not tracking well, while others were more stressed when they had to work longer hours. However we can see that the mood of many in the team improved in the last few days of the Sprint.

The Scrum Maser should keep any sticky-notes, marked with where and how they originated, as these should provide a useful source for potential improvement ideas later in the Retrospective.

Remembering what happened

Once the team feels safe enough to contribute and have shared how they feel, they should move on to the next stage, reviewing how effective they were and looking for any patterns that emerge.

There are many techniques for this stage of a Retrospective, mostly based around a structured game that guides participants to explore how effective their practices, techniques and activities were.

Celebrate as well as commiserate

For the morale of the team, it is important to form a rounded assessment. When teams have achieved something good, they should call that out and celebrate it. When something did not go well, they should be confident in admitting that, and agreeing that it was an experience they do not want to repeat.

Scrum anti-patterns

As fun as some of these games may appear, their real purpose is to identify what practices, techniques or activities need attention.

When we adopt something new and repeat it successfully, we are establishing a pattern for ourselves and others to follow. Adopting Scrum as an approach to product development requires a shift in mindset, and there is a risk that any new practice will be wrongly adopted or changed so much that it becomes an **anti-pattern**.

There are too many examples of Scrum anti-patterns to attempt a complete list, but a few examples include:

- Continually adding things to the Definition of Ready means the team are pushing for too much to be done up front.

- Using the Daily Scrum as a status report meeting means the team are not thinking about progress or daily plans.

- Tracking individual utilization, rather than overall throughput means the team are not thinking like a team.

- Starting new work when there is still work in progress means the team are preferring busyness over progress.

- Adding columns to the Scrum Board means the team are focusing on individual disciplines and adding hand-over points.

- Focusing too tightly on Sprint outputs runs the risk of neglecting overall progress of the Release.

Explore and identify subjects for concern

Most Retrospective games are designed to help teams make sense of what they experienced in the last Sprint – the first step before deciding on any team improvements:

1 Prepare the playing area on a whiteboard and place any sticky-notes from earlier exercises in the appropriate space

2 Agree a fixed time, typically five minutes, for participants to write their points on sticky-notes, usually in silence

3 When the time is up, take it in turns to bring sticky-notes up to the whiteboard

- Read out and briefly explain each point

- Place the sticky-note in the appropriate space

- Keep discussion only to ensure it is understood

4 Once everyone has placed their sticky-notes and nobody has thought of anything else significant they want to add, the team should move onto the next stage of the Retrospective – thinking about what actions they can take

Games to identify areas for analysis

The following games will help identify areas that teams may want to address:

- **Stop, Start, Continue**: Split the whiteboard into these three columns for the sticky-notes – variations of this game include **Liked, Learned, Lacked**; **KALM** (keep, add, less, and more), and **WWW** (worked well, kinda worked, and didn't work).

- **Open the Box**: Draw a box in the middle of the whiteboard with three lines radiating out, mark the spaces between the spokes as remove, add, and recycle.

- **Sail-Boat**: Draw a sail-boat on the whiteboard with wind, rocks, and an anchor – the boat is the team, the wind is what enabled their progress, the anchor is what held them back, and the rocks are any risks that still lie ahead.

While it is natural for teams to start discussing or arguing over individual points, this will slow down the process, and should be left to the final stage.

To keep Retrospectives fresh and even fun, the same game should not be used for more than a couple of Sprints.

Making sense of it all

Aside from team-building, a key purpose of the Retrospective is to agree on actions that mitigate or resolve Impediments before they become bigger challenges in future Sprints.

Making sense of all the points with affinity-grouping

Following the exercises in the preceding topics, the team will typically have a wall full of sticky-notes. (This will be too many to identify potential improvement actions.) Before they embark on that activity, the team first needs to collect them into groups.

Affinity-grouping is an effective technique for identifying general themes quickly, which are then easier to prioritize and work with:

1 Set a time limit for the activity – usually no more than five minutes – and stop when the time has been used up

2 Gather around the whiteboard and take turns moving a sticky-note next to another dealing with a similar concern

3 If this results in too many groups, try a second round – usually of a shorter duration – to combine similar groups

4 Draw lines around the sticky-notes to identify the groups

5 Decide what theme each group represents and write a name or short phrase next to it

In completing this activity, a team should be capable of identifying no more than around nine themes. The team at Dante's generated five themes from the issues they identified.

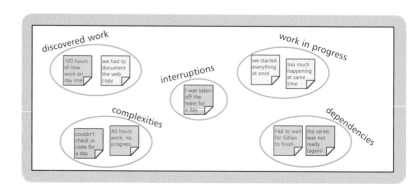

Once the team has a reasonable number of themes identified, they then need to select the most important – one that the team can work on, and perhaps another that needs to be escalated.

Agreeing on high priority items by dot-voting

Dot-voting is an effective technique for quickly agreeing on a priority, in which team members choose how to distribute a limited number of dots amongst the identified themes. Some people play a similar game using tokens or toy money which people can *spend* on the themes:

1 Set and keep to a time limit for this exercise – five minutes is typically sufficient

2 Hand out a limited number of sticky dots, typically just three per person

3 Gather around the whiteboard and place dots next to whatever themes seem important to each participant – choosing whether to place all three next to a single theme, to split them two-plus-one, or spread all three separately

4 Once all dots have been placed or the time has run out, count the number of dots to identify which themes have been chosen as the top three

If too many themes end up with the same number of dots, give everyone one more dot and repeat the exercise. The team at Dante's chose discovered work, with 10 dots, and interruptions, with six, as the themes to focus on most.

Hot tip

If there are no sticky dots, it is possible to use a whiteboard marker pen to place three dots.

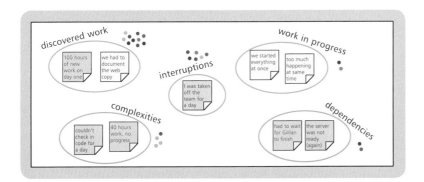

Understanding the root cause

Once the team has agreed on the top theme to tackle, they should consider the root causes. Rather than just solving the symptoms, it is better to invest a little more time to find what caused them.

The team needs to consider different aspects of the problem. In doing this, they may uncover a more deep-seated problem that they then decide is better to tackle.

There are two common techniques used for root-cause analysis:

Five Whys
The **Five Whys** is a recursive brainstorming technique to uncover the root cause: for each reason, ask again why that occurred, and then again why the reasons for that occurred. This may be completed in as few as three rounds or it may take many more.

Fishbone Diagram
If you need a more structured alternative, the **Fishbone Diagram** prompts teams to think within potential categories:

1 Draw the Fishbone Diagram (see Dante's example below), write the theme at the head, and label the main bones with categories – place, procedure, people, policies, etc.

2 Brainstorm potential causes for the theme that could originate from each category

3 For each potential cause, explore the potential reasons, adding more branches off the bones as needed

4 Look for issues appearing in more than one branch, or those which the team feel are strong factors – use dot-voting if needed – and take the results of this into the next stage

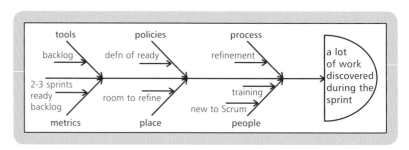

Taking action to improve

Having identified the most important theme to tackle, and agreeing what the root causes are, the team should now work together to agree what an appropriate change might be.

Often the solution will be clear once the problem is clear. However, with more complex problems the team might prefer to brainstorm alternative ideas with sticky-notes on a whiteboard. If there are many possible ideas, the team should repeat the affinity-grouping and dot-voting exercises to come to an agreed solution.

This approach, of iteratively creating then selecting options for identifying problems and for exploring solutions, is very similar to the Double Diamond Design Thinking approach (see page 32).

Keeping actions SMART

In Chapter Six, we saw that tasks for Product Backlog Items should be SMART; the same is true for team improvements:

- **Specific**: everyone on the team understands what is required.

- **Measurable**: it is clear what a successful outcome looks like.

- **Actionable**: the team are able to implement it.

- **Relevant**: it is clear how the outcome resolves the root causes.

- **Time-boxed**: an agreed cap on how long the team should spend on it – definitely less than a single Sprint.

Making the team improvement visible

After co-designing a solution in the Retrospective on which they agree, the team should display the team improvement on their Scrum Board. This means they can see it easily, every day. Should they realize that they cannot implement the solution by themselves, they should escalate whatever constraint is limiting them as an Organizational Impediment (see page 150).

The team at Dante's chose to experiment by not accepting any Product Backlog Item larger than 13 Story points. Their Scrum Master, Joe, knew instinctively that this would be too large, but realized that the team should learn this by themselves rather than just be told.

They also agreed to refine their work further ahead and asked the Product Owner to involve them with the Discovery Team.

Scrum Teams move through three stages of growth, typically portrayed with the martial arts term *Shu-Ha-Ri* (see Chapter One).

High-performance coaching

It takes time for teams to become proficient, and even longer to reach high performance. The Sprint Retrospective is one of the key ways that the team can explore ways of becoming better.

Taking steps toward higher performance

Continual improvement tends to be incremental in nature, but becoming a high-performing team requires more significant change. This normally requires insight and coaching from outside the Delivery Team itself, and is one reason that having a dedicated person in the role of Scrum Master is particularly beneficial.

The Scrum Master is responsible for their own ongoing development, and particularly how teams improve their performance. This is typically through self-paced learning from books, conferences, webinars, visits to other organizations, and community events.

In their Retrospective, teams consider how they feel, how effective they have been, and what problems they faced. The Scrum Master should also highlight any high-performance factors for discussion.

High-performance behaviors

A number of high-performance behaviors have been described throughout the book:

- **Teamwork**: the team believes that they succeed or fail together; there are no individual winners.

- **Courage**: good teams speak openly and admit when they don't know the answer or get stuck.

- **Autonomy**: the team have experienced the Product Owner trusting them to deliver what they say and when.

- **Ownership**: the team understand and feel accountable for any flaw or imperfection in the product.

- **Commitment**: high-performance requires the whole team to stay committed and motivated.

- **Focus**: the team's work comes only from a single Product Backlog, as prioritized by one Product Owner.

High-performance techniques

Several high-performance techniques have been explored across each chapter:

- **Ready Backlog**: ensure Product Backlog Items meet the Definition of Ready for two to three Sprints ahead.

- **Limit work in progress**: focus on delivering throughput of value rather than just keeping busy.

- **Swarming**: everyone works together to complete higher priority items before anyone starts lower priority ones.

- **Stretching**: the team challenges itself to improve, to deliver more and with higher quality.

- **Release frequency**: the team are able to release software as often as needed, every Sprint or more frequently.

- **No estimates**: the team consistently breaks work down to be small enough to minimize risk and complexity – without sizing.

High-performance metrics

Teams should regularly review their metrics and seek ways of adjusting towards higher performance targets, such as:

- **Focus**: no more than 15% of the team's capacity should be used for work outside the Product Backlog.

- **Quality**: the team produces fewer than 10 defects per 100 Story points.

- **Throughput**: delivery of value should be improving or consistent and predictable – barring significant events.

- **Completion ratio**: the team regularly meets their Sprint forecast with over 90% accuracy (i.e. +/- 10% Story points).

- **Stability**: the team stays and grows stronger together, changing no more than one person every three months.

- **Overtime**: less than 5% of the team's time in a Sprint comes from overtime.

An Impediment is anything that blocks the team from completing their work (see page 120).

Organizational Impediments

An Organizational Impediment is any constraint that has a repeated and ongoing effect, often on multiple teams. Part of the Scrum Master's role is to help the organization understand how to achieve the most from adopting Scrum to develop products. The Scrum Master advocates on behalf their team, as these Impediments are typically too big to be resolved by a single team.

In an ideal system, work is able to flow as needed to match customer demand, with any variance small enough to be absorbed. Any constraints that cause work to speed up or slow down too much can lead to waste like stockpiling or stoppage, and ultimately higher costs and dissatisfied customers.

Constraints are normal

Constraints arise naturally in all processes and often help regulate or govern the flow. In Scrum, for example, the Sprint acts as a natural cycle of governance. While the need to start and stop on a regular basis results in some non-development time, this is used for preventive maintenance (i.e. the Sprint Retrospective).

When a constraint overly impedes flow, however, it has become an Impediment that needs to be understood, mitigated or resolved.

Organization anti-patterns

Most Organizational Impediments are unique to an organization. However, there are common dysfunctional patterns. For example:

- **Measuring the wrong thing**: focusing key performance indicators on individual disciplines discourages collaboration.

- **Centralized processes**: imposing standardized processes draws resources away from areas that add value.

- **Functional silos**: continuing to work in specialist groups creates barriers for communication.

- **Poor training**: when learning is not a priority, there is often fire-fighting and heroic efforts rather than collaboration.

- **Superficial adoption**: adopting Scrum solely to develop products faster misses out on the bigger benefits of adaptability.

- **Local optimization**: improving an unconstrained area will result in no real improvement to end-to-end flow, and will likely cause more problems where there are constraints.

How to handle Organizational Impediments

There is a five-step process to handle Organizational Impediments:

This five-step process comes from the *Theory of Constraints* and can be applied to constraints at any level.

1 **Identify the constraint**: when an Impediment is escalated, make sure the root cause has been identified – for example, delays in deployment might be caused by applying plan-driven Release management approaches

2 **Focus the constraint**: identify and remove any activities that impede the throughput of value – for example, if a quality checkpoint is no longer necessary due to testing within the Sprint, it should be abandoned

3 **Support the constraint**: if this is already operating at its optimum, adjust the flow of work to avoid becoming overloaded – for example, some of the quality checkpoint testing could be moved into the Sprint

4 **Strengthen the constraint**: assuming the team is still blocked from delivering value, consider increasing capacity or improving capability – for example, training the team on how to automate tests or recruiting a test automation engineer to join the team

5 **Prevent inertia**: when this has been successfully resolved, measures should be put in place to ensure that it doesn't reappear, then focus should shift to finding the next one

By working through these five steps, the Scrum Master will help the organization shift gears from a fire-fighting mode to one of continual improvement (see page 152).

Don't get overwhelmed

Making Organizational Impediments transparent is intended to be an uncomfortable process. While some Impediments will be easier to resolve, many are large and seem too complex. To avoid becoming overwhelmed, establish the habit of capturing each Impediment as a RIDA (see page 120) and managing them like any other risk. Break a large Impediment down, to make it possible to work on it progressively.

Lean change management

Scrum Masters often want to help their organization evolve from reactive problem-solving to continual improvement. They need the support of leadership and a framework for how to approach it.

Forming a Delivery Leadership Team

In larger organizations, the Scrum Master is seldom able to achieve this by themselves. They may not be able to choose which problems to fix or may not have enough influence to resolve them.

At this point, they should look to form a team of senior leaders who are motivated to continually improve how the organization uses Scrum. This team should represent all areas involved in discovering and delivering the product, plus those who support it.

Selecting the right level of leadership

Take care to select the right level of leadership. Leaders who are too senior will definitely bring attention, but may become disengaged if the change is too small. On the other hand, involving people with insufficient authority will lead to frustration.

Start with the scope – does it affect the whole organization, a single division, a portfolio of products, or a single product? This determines the highest level of leadership required.

For organizational change, engage the Chief Executive roles; for divisional change, the vice presidents or directors; and for a portfolio, the affected managers will be sufficient.

Leadership advocacy for Scrum

Leaders will vary in their experience and advocacy, from the most engaged and positive to those who could act against the change:

- **Innovators**: very experienced and positive – thought leaders.

- **Champions**: know Scrum well and will keenly advocate for it.

- **Workhorses**: learned Scrum by doing it – mostly positive.

- **Bandwagon**: support it while they have something to gain.

- **Cowboys**: opportunists – easily swayed either for or against.

- **Deceivers**: appear to support Scrum while undermining it.

- **Deniers**: challenge that there will be any benefit at all.

While a Delivery Leadership Team should consist of the strongest advocates, Innovators are rare inside organizations, and there are never enough Champions. Seek out the most engaged in the Workhorse and Bandwagon groups and then coach as Champions.

A lean change framework for continual improvement

The Scrum Master will need to coach the Delivery Leadership Team in adopting a feedback-driven framework for organization change:

1 **Backlog**: build the Backlog from Impediments that have been escalated, plus any other opportunities identified

2 **Triage**: use the Risk score (impact and likelihood) to select which one represents the biggest challenge

3 **Analyze**: try to form a working hypothesis that could explain what has happened from what can be observed

4 **Safe-to-fail**: look for the minimum viable change that could resolve this – simple enough to finish within three months, and small enough to do no lasting damage

5 **Prioritize**: if more than one change, assess the effort and impact of each, to find the highest impact for the lowest effort

6 **Run**: engage people affected by the change in its implementation and transparently monitor progress

7 **Validate**: if the change failed, roll it back or quietly drop it – if it worked, think about how to build on it

8 **Repeat**: check if the Impediment has been resolved, and if so, whether it is still the biggest challenge – if not, then close it out and find the next challenge

After tackling all the Impediments to adopting Scrum, the Delivery Leadership Team should stay together. Their focus should shift to continually improving how the organization delivers a reliable flow of value and generates learning and useful feedback.

Don't forget

Just as with developing a product, break large items of work into smaller chunks to deliver iteratively, and be ready to stop when enough value has been delivered.

153

Start an agile transformation

By helping Delivery Teams handle Impediments, the Scrum Master guides them through incremental team improvements. They should also be drawing on good practice to identify topics on which they can coach them to achieve higher performance.

So too, the Scrum Master guides the organization through improvements that resolve their systemic Impediments. They should also be drawing on good organization practice – instead of waiting for problems, they should look further ahead to identify opportunities for substantive improvement.

The start of the transformation

Problem-solving and continual improvement are effective forms for change, for the scale of problem they are designed to solve. However, as soon as the Scrum Master moves beyond resolving Organizational Impediments and starts to aim for more significant change, they start to shift the organization out of a mode of continual improvement and into one of transformation.

Transformation is a far more challenging form of change. Firstly, transformational change is complex. The outcome is often not known in advance, but rather has to emerge through trial and error (see *Cynefin Framework*, page 11). This means that it suits a feedback-driven approach.

Secondly, major transformation shifts the nature of change, away from changing **how we do** something to changing **who we are**. Often new behaviors are required and culture must change.

This makes the process unpredictable and potentially scary for many people in the organization – for executives as well as frontline workers. Lack of information and stress will likely lead to high levels of resistance, and has been a fundamental reason that so many transformations do not succeed.

While embarking on a transformation is a significant and risky challenge, there are huge rewards from creating fundamental shifts in the way people think as well as the way they work.

In attempting such a challenge, the Scrum Master has to build on their work in establishing the Delivery Leadership Team and in adopting a lean change framework for tackling large change in small slices. They themselves are transformed, and are now acting more in the role of an Enterprise Agile Coach.

Thankfully, there is a reliable six-step framework for improving the odds of success:

1) Form a Transformation Leadership Team

The Scrum Master should now guide the Delivery Leadership Team through establishing a new purpose – as a team to lead the transformation. If necessary, engage with more senior stakeholders as the scope for the transformation will likely be broader.

The purpose of the Transformation Leadership Team is to provide guidance and support through the transformation. They should be able to build support and handle resistance with middle-management, and move the organization's language from planning and budgeting to a concern for flow of value.

2) Agreeing a clear end vision

Just as with product development, our approach to transformation should be flexible, driven by feedback, and allow for adaptation. In Chapter Five, we were introduced to the five levels of product planning that start at a high-level and progressively become more defined, as understanding evolves and the team gets closer to doing the work.

The Transformation Leadership Team starts by establishing a clear vision of the end-state they want to work toward. This acts as their *true north* to keep any change aligned. By reference to what good practice looks like in other organizations, they should think about how they need to be structured, how they should govern their work, and what they should measure to determine if they are successful.

They should identify a pilot area, possibly as small as just one product, to test their model, and adapt as required. However, this cannot be an isolated change. It must be part of a broader organizational roll-out.

For product organizations, you should base your model on the twin focuses of customer alignment and product development.

Review the scaled frameworks covered in Chapter Ten, and select the one that seems to best match. In many ways, it doesn't matter if it is not entirely right the first time, as by piloting you should get early feedback so that you can make adjustments before rolling out to the wider organization.

Beware

In embarking on a journey of agile transformation, keep the approach lean and agile; do not adopt overly planned change management practices.

...cont'd

3) Developing a 12-month rolling Roadmap

As a transformation is a long-term exercise, it helps to communicate to the organization roughly what will be happening, when, and for how long. Based on their end vision, the Transformation Leadership Team needs to establish their Roadmap for transformation.

They should identify the key capabilities their organization needs, and allow time to develop those throughout the year ahead. While large scale transformation efforts typically require more than a year, most employees will struggle with thinking too far ahead, so 12 months is an effective planning horizon.

Where possible, it helps to select a pilot area to start introducing change, while keeping in mind the need to roll this out to the broader organization later. Consider what teams might need to be formed, where they will come from, and any training and coaching they need.

To ensure that this is feedback-driven, time should also be allowed for establishing a baseline for how the transformation will be monitored and reported.

Finally, the Transformation Leadership Team should plan for regular updates on progress, be ready to change the plan as necessary, and remember that this is a rolling Roadmap. As time passes and outcomes are achieved, new outcomes are added to the end so that there is always a longer term picture.

4) Planning activities for 90 days

With a Vision and Roadmap in place, the Transformation Leadership Team needs to start planning the work required to develop those capabilities. They should start meeting periodically to plan ahead. Three months is enough to allow any changes implemented to start showing some results so that they can reassess their Vision.

Create a 90-day plan that shows week by week what training and coaching will be done with each part of the organization, what resources are required, how assessments will be taken, and when to communicate progress.

With enough support and more coaches, it should be possible to make more than one change per quarter, and to work with a rolling 90-day plan.

5) Checking in every 30 days

As they progress through the 90-day plan, the Transformation Leadership Team must regularly assess progress and re-plan when required. Although they may choose to meet as frequently as weekly to provide guidance and triage new Impediments, they should set time aside once per month as a formal checkpoint. This will allow them to focus on the metrics being collected, which should show how well the transformation is progressing.

Metrics are critical for how the Transformation Leadership Team make decisions, and should show how far they have gone and whether anything is going off-track. The metrics chosen should have a clear and obvious link to the capabilities being developed, encouraging and reinforcing the desired change.

Typical transformation metrics include: time to market, Release frequency, stabilization time, Backlog readiness, team stability, Feature throughput, defect density, and agile maturity.

6) Keeping people informed and helping them feel safe

While adopting agile practices is about changing what an organization does, an agile transformation is more about changing who the organization is. The shift from **doing agile** to **becoming agile** marks the move from the *Shu* to the *Ha* stages mentioned in Chapter One. As it requires shifts in mindset and behaviors as well as practices and techniques, it has a much larger impact on people.

Two things are critical in ensuring that any changes are well received and stick. Firstly, the Transformation Leadership Team must keep everyone informed about what is planned and how it is progressing. This helps people anticipate the impact and timing of change on them. Secondly, they should seek to engage and involve people actively in the transformation process itself. This helps people associate themselves more with the change, to see it as their change rather than something that could threaten them.

Closing thoughts

Embarking on a journey of agile transformation in any organization is a significant undertaking. While these steps have been proven to implement a framework for successful outcomes, unless your Transformation Leadership Team includes any experienced thought-leaders, it is advisable to get some outside guidance to get this going. Good luck.

Summary

- The Sprint finally ends with the Sprint Retrospective – immediately after the Sprint Review – where the team think about how well the past Sprint went and consider any improvements they could make in the coming Sprint.

- Sprint Retrospectives are time-boxed to 90 minutes for a typical two-week Sprint – pro-rata lower or higher for shorter or longer Sprint durations.

- The retrospective is normally held in a separate room, where team members will feel safe talking more openly.

- The Scrum Master will lead the team through a number of exercises to explore what happened, identify any repeating patterns of issues, and highlight which are the most critical.

- The team should collaborate on understanding the root cause and agreeing on team improvement actions to tackle them.

- The Scrum Master should also identify opportunities to coach the team towards higher performance.

- Any issues that the team cannot resolve for themselves are likely to be Organizational Impediments.

- The Scrum Master should form a Delivery Leadership Team and coach them in continual improvement practices to work effectively on resolving the Organizational Impediments escalated to them.

- Where more significant change is required, the Scrum Master should consider reforming the Delivery Leadership Team into a Transformation Leadership Team, and guide them through a lean change approach to organizational change.

- The Transformation Leadership Team should endeavor to keep everyone informed about their Roadmap for change and how well it is progressing – this helps people anticipate the impact and timing of change on them.

- They should also involve people actively in the transformation process itself – this helps people associate themselves more with the change, to see it as their change rather than something that could threaten them.

10 Scaling Scrum beyond one team

This chapter looks at how Scrum can work beyond one team; handling dependencies with other Scrum Teams, non-product teams, deployment teams, Governance, and strategy.

Scrum beyond a single team

Organizations often start with a single Delivery Team, and then find that one team is not enough or that the team becomes dependent on other parts of the organization. This chapter reviews a number of typical scenarios, and considers how the team and their organization might adapt to deal with these.

Working with other teams to develop a product

Development on complex products often takes longer. To improve throughput, most organizations think they need to scale up. Rather than have a single team work on a product, they commit several teams to work together from the same Product Backlog.

Complexities in deploying work from multiple teams

In large organizations, it is often not possible for Scrum Teams to deploy the product direct to customers themselves. This can be due to regulation, internal policy, or simply custom. Such organizations typically have other teams that take the work from Scrum Teams to integrate, test, and deploy to the customer.

Working with legacy system teams

Organizations that are well-established typically operate their new products alongside legacy systems. Coordination and planning is critical to ensuring that Scrum Teams can complete work that is dependent on legacy systems.

Sharing specialist roles between multiple teams

Delivery Teams should have all the skills required to design, build, test, and deploy their product. While individuals are encouraged to be multi-disciplined, some skills are highly specialized and used so infrequently that the team chooses to rely instead on specialists who often support a number of teams.

Managing scarce funds across multiple products

Large organizations typically have multiple products or product lines, and many teams to develop and support them. They need a robust approach to coordinating and planning work without slowing down throughput. They need a mechanism for selecting, guiding, and validating work that ensures a reasonable flow combined with just enough oversight.

The following pages explore each of these scenarios in more depth, explaining the steps you can take. The chapter closes with a look at the most common frameworks for using Scrum at scale.

Multiple Delivery Teams

When you need to scale up development capacity for a product, you can form additional Scrum Teams and have them work from the same Product Backlog.

Forming additional Scrum Teams

As the need for more teams becomes clear, it can be tempting to take some people from the existing team. It takes time for a new team to become productive (see page 26). Each time someone joins or leaves a team, their productivity is set back as they adjust.

Rather than break a well performing team to help form new teams, it would be better to leave that team in place and form the new teams from scratch. There will still be opportunities for sharing good practice and experience between the teams as they collaborate on the same product.

Do not form new teams by breaking up existing ones that are performing well.

Working from the same Product Backlog

In order that deliverables from each team can be well-coordinated, the teams should all work from the same Product Backlog. This ensures that they work to the same priorities and have a shared understanding of the Vision and Roadmap.

When teams are developing work that will be combined into the same product, it is also vital that they work from a shared Definition of Done. This ensures that they build to the same standards and a common set of deliverables.

Synchronization and planning

In bringing multiple teams together, there are also certain aspects of Scrum itself that have to be carefully adapted:

- **Synchronized Sprints**: so that the planning and delivery of work can be coordinated, the Sprints for all teams should be of the same duration (i.e. two weeks) and start on the same day.

- **Combined Scrum events**: so that teams understand the work they are each doing and the impact they could have on each other, some aspects of the planning and review events should be combined (see page 170 for information on scaled frameworks).

- **Collaboration between teams**: during each Sprint, teams should maintain constant awareness and coordination of progress and potential Impediments, the following topic suggests one approach for this.

Scrum of Scrums coordination

For products that require multiple teams to work on the same Product Backlog, it is vital that the progress of each team remains synchronized and known across all teams. This is especially true when there are dependencies between the teams.

The Scrum of Scrums

One common approach is for one person from each team to act as a representative to other teams, in a joint event known as a Scrum of Scrums, to review key Risks, Impediments, Dependencies, and Assumptions. This normally takes place straight after all teams have completed their Daily Scrums.

The role of team representative

The team as a whole selects who their representative for the Scrum of Scrums should be. This should be someone who can adequately represent the team on the key challenges of the day, so this responsibility will likely change day-to-day and Sprint-to-Sprint.

Depending on the context, the representative may be a member of the Delivery Team, the Scrum Master, or on rare occasions even a Line Manager (e.g. for Impediments related to Capacity).

For example: challenges early in development are most likely to be technical, so teams would send someone strong in that technical area. Later challenges are more likely to be around integration or testing, so teams would call on someone with those skills.

Frequency and duration

The collective teams should determine for themselves how frequently they should meet for a Scrum of Scrums. On low risk developments this may be just once or twice a week, but most often it takes place every day, immediately after the individual Daily Scrum.

Like the Daily Scrum (see Chapter Seven), the Scrum of Scrums is also time-boxed to 15 minutes, so it cannot be a forum for resolving any challenges identified. However, on more complex developments, not resolving an Impediment immediately may delay the work of several teams. As this may be the only time in the day when those specific team representatives will be together, it may be prudent to reserve up to an hour. Once the initial quarter hour is used, they can separate and use the remaining time to collaborate as necessary to resolve outstanding Impediments.

162

Hot tip

Being a team's representative for the Scrum of Scrums should not be seen as a permanent appointment.

Number of people

The Scrum of Scrums would normally involve a representative from every team working on the same Product Backlog. This may make it unworkable for products with a large number of teams.

In such situations, organizations often resort to another layer, whereby a representative from each Scrum of Scrums would meet with others to coordinate at a more abstract level.

The additional layers increase the time it takes to communicate and manage Impediments and Dependencies across the entire team. However, it is more effective than attempting the same activity with 30-50 team representatives.

The scaled frameworks for Scrum considered later in this chapter have a range of approaches for how to run an equivalent to the Scrum of Scrums across multiple teams.

The Scrum of Scrums questions

The purpose of the Scrum of Scrums is to enable transparency and focus around Risks, Impediments, Dependencies, and Assumptions. As with the Daily Scrum sessions for each team, the Scrum of Scrums achieves this with three simple questions that help keep discussion focused and maintain momentum.

In the Daily Scrum, the three questions focus on progress with Stories, Defects, and Tasks in their Sprint Backlog (see page 110).

Those attending the Scrum of Scrums answer three questions around the Risks, Impediments, Dependencies, and Assumptions they have identified or are already tracking:

- What has my team resolved that unblocks other teams?

- What will my team work to resolve next?

- Has my team identified any new Risks, Impediments, Dependencies, or Assumptions that could block another team?

Tracking outstanding cross-team Impediments

As has been noted, it is vital that all Risks, Impediments, Dependencies, and Assumptions are actively tracked. This is most often achieved through maintaining a shared Risk Board (see Chapter Eight), that can act as a Backlog for the Scrum of Scrums.

Beware

As tempting as it is to start discussing possible solutions, it is critical that these three questions are answered from all teams first.

Deploying product at scale

Creating a potentially shippable Product Increment is challenging when several teams work together, or where they are integrating with environments not under their control. They can mitigate these by how they time Integration, Verification, and Deployment.

Deploying once per Release

For mature products in well-established markets, rather than being faced with updates every two weeks or more often, customers typically prefer a steadier program of enhancements which they can anticipate, and for which they can prepare.

Organizations serve these customers better by deploying less frequently, just at the end of a Release. While a Release can be any duration (see Chapter Five), it is fairly typical to plan four Releases per year, or once per quarter.

Integrating and verifying once per Release

When organizations choose to deploy less frequently, it is tempting for them to leave Integration and Verification until they have completed development. While that can appear efficient, it creates a separate stage for work to go through. This creates a bottleneck, slows down flow, and leads to more plan-driven behaviors. It is also inherently more risky.

Even when deploying quarterly, there are major benefits to starting the Integration and Verification of work as early as possible, especially when dealing with multiple teams.

Integrating and verifying in the following Sprint

To avoid a bottleneck towards the end of a Release, it can be better to integrate the work of one Sprint during the Sprint that follows. This is often undertaken by a separate System or Integration Team.

While this means there will be some Integration and Verification left to do after development is complete, that can usually be completed in a single stabilization Sprint (see page 125).

However, whenever we integrate work, there is always a risk that something will go wrong. Any problems discovered must now be classed as Defects (see Chapter Seven), as the Integration is not in the same Sprint. This will lead to more overheads on handling the problem. The team that will resolve the Defect has to either drop work they committed to for that Sprint, or delay resolution of the Defect to a following Sprint.

Integrating and verifying in the same Sprint

A key benefit of Scrum as a product development framework is that work is developed, tested, and documented altogether in the same Sprint. This is what enables fast feedback, potentially deploying a Product Increment each and every Sprint.

Even if your organization chooses to deploy only once per quarter, you can still mitigate the risks discussed above by including the Integration and Verification of work in the same Sprint as the development. This tends to challenge many of the systems and processes organizations have in place, so is typically only successful in those organizations reaching a level of maturity and confidence with Scrum and the technical practices.

To reinforce this approach, teams will include Integration and Verification in their Definition of Done. They will need to focus on how they coordinate their work during the Sprint, so that they are able to successfully integrate as they complete each of the story PBIs in their separate Sprint Backlogs. This requires a higher level of coordination and collaboration than even the Scrum of Scrums, as described on pages 162-163.

Integrating and verifying continuously

Finally, smart organizations opt to integrate work as soon as it is finished. With software development, this can mean that a new build of the complete software is automatically triggered when code is checked into the repository. Once the software build is completed, a number of automated regression tests are then run to verify that all the existing functionality still works as intended.

This does not yet verify the new functionality – this will be added to the automated test suite once it has been confirmed as meeting its Acceptance Criteria.

Should the software fail to build or the automated tests not pass, the check-in is classed as *breaking the build* and the whole team receive an alert in a very clear and obvious way. Some teams choose to have a light flash or a sound played to draw their attention.

Continuous Integration and Verification is part of the suite of automated activities required for DevOps (see page 127).

Working with non-Scrum roles

As you scale up your product development capabilities, they often separate out development, support, and specialists into different functions or departments.

Unless Scrum Teams are working on an entirely new product, they typically have to give some attention to the complexities and dependencies of integrating into an environment containing services that are developed and maintained by other groups.

This heightens the need for good coordination and collaboration; even more so when those other areas have not adopted Scrum as their preferred way of working (for example, legacy systems).

Working with plan-driven teams

One of the major challenges for Scrum Teams working with those following a plan-driven approach, is the difference in the timing and the level of planning.

Typically, on plan-driven projects all activities, milestones and dates are detailed up front before any work starts.

Scrum Teams, however, start with a conceptual plan: the Product Roadmap (see page 69). This sets out probable dates for Features, well before detailed commitment is made. Work is not defined down to the Task level until the Sprint Planning of the Sprint in which the work will be done, to allow for changing requirements.

This means when Scrum Teams and plan-driven teams want to discuss their inter-dependencies, they are working from different perspectives – which leads to many misunderstandings.

Understanding Critical Path

Plan-driven teams invest significant time up front looking at their **Critical Path** – the sequence or chain of activities that is at the highest risk if anything gets delayed.

They look at best-case and worst-case scenarios, by linking each activity with any others on which they are dependent. Then they have to work out the earliest and the latest that they could start and finish each activity. This is also referred to as the Program Evaluation and Review Technique (or PERT).

Understanding this constraint becomes a powerful tool in negotiating dependency dates.

Don't forget

Legacy systems are built on older technology and typically maintained following more plan-driven approaches.

The next step after the Product Roadmap is Release Planning. Although this will be in more detail, it has a shorter time horizon. The Roadmap looks ahead for 12-18 months, while the Release Plan typically looks ahead for only three months. It does map Features and Stories to Sprints, but this is still liable to change up to the Sprint Planning event for each of the Sprints.

This means the Scrum Team can establish at the beginning of the year, roughly when they will need the plan-driven team to get involved. Four times a year, they can then have a more detailed discussion of what is needed that quarter, while there is still flexibility in precisely which Sprint something is built.

To ensure the Scrum Team can work effectively with plan-driven teams, it is vital to start communication early and keep it going.

Sharing specialist roles between multiple teams

Although Delivery Teams should ideally have all the skills required to build and deploy (see Chapter Two), in complex environments there are often highly specialized skills – such as user experience (UX) design or database administration.

A team heavily reliant on UX, for example, could choose to employ a designer full-time. However, these capabilities are most typically needed infrequently and in short bursts. In such circumstances, an organization is likely to have a specialist team.

In highly-scaled environments they might choose to bring together one person from each specialist discipline into a **Shared Services Team**, dedicated to supporting all the teams on a product.

Wherever they are, Delivery Teams need to able to draw on their specialist skills in a timely manner. The Scrum Team needs to identify the need for these specialists in enough time for them to complete their work and enable the team to start when intended.

Where the specialists are working in the same environment as the Delivery Teams, it may be possible to create tasks for them during Backlog Refinement. That way, their work can also be seen and tracked transparently.

This is one of the reasons that teams should strive to refine Product Backlog Items at least two to three Sprints ahead of when they intend to start the work (see Chapter Four).

Governing work at scale

All organizations typically want to achieve far more than is possible with their limited funds, resources, time, and people. This creates an environment in which departments and executives have to compete to get their product developed.

To manage this effectively, you need light governance constraints on development work to ensure that it is all strategically aligned, timed for sufficient throughput, and built to earn a return on investment. Governance helps this by filtering what gets done – confirming that it is fit for purpose and meets the needs of your customer and of your organization – then maintaining oversight. These key decision points, by which work is approved to progress from one stage to the next, are referred to as Gates.

Stage Gate governance *(decision diamonds between activities)*

Gates usually involve senior executives and are often spread across locations and times. This can lead to Governance Gates becoming a drawn-out multi-step process taking days, if not weeks, to come to a decision. While typical in plan-driven projects, this is too heavy-handed and slow for a product developed with Scrum.

Historically, product development has been organized and funded through capital projects. However, organizations are increasingly shifting to product development as a permanent operationally-funded function. While such organizations will typically no longer run projects, they still need an approach to Governance that allows them to approve and track work.

Instead of projects, work needs to be approved and benefits tracked at the highest level on the Product Backlog: the Epic. For this reason, the Epic will often have additional information, such as the Business Case that justifies why the Epic should be built.

Lean Governance

A new approach to Governance is also required – one that satisfies these concerns without breaking the rules of the Scrum framework. One that is leaner and more effective.

Hot tip

Governance should be primarily about balancing the selection of initiatives in which to invest, with just enough oversight to ensure they deliver what is promised.

Beware

Avoid making time-sensitive decisions by email discussion. This often results in a simple decision taking several days that could have been agreed in minutes in person.

To make Governance lean and effective, the right timing, preparation, tools, and processes are required:

- The timing of Governance decisions should be sensitive to the frequency of development Sprints.

- Governance decisions must include all critical roles at the same time, to avoid delays by chasing people for their feedback and decisions.

- The status and progress of all work should be visualized: whether new, prioritized for a future release, currently in progress, or recently completed.

- Executives assess all this work against the same criteria of strategic fit, customer need, feasibility, cost, profitability, etc.

- Any work failing the criteria should either be stopped and canceled, sent back for further research, or by exception approved with conditions attached.

- Approved work would then be prioritized against all other approved work for impact, effort, and urgency (see page 72).

- Depending on its relative priority, work may be planned into the Roadmap for a future Release, started immediately if new and urgent, or continued if reviewed while In Progress.

- When funds or resources need to be freed up for new work of a higher priority than work currently In Progress, the decision might be to stop and deploy what has been developed so far, to temporarily put the current work on hold, or even to cancel and drop it altogether.

Governance can become leaner by keeping reviews simpler, having all information at your fingertips, and ensuring everyone is adequately prepared.

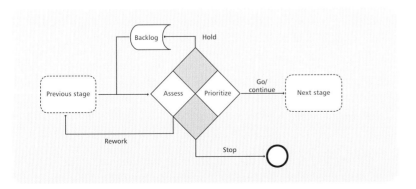

Scaled frameworks for Scrum

Three frameworks have emerged that support large organizations wanting to understand how they should adopt Scrum at scale.

Summarized over the following four pages, each has a different focus, and you should consider which might work for you. Large-Scale Scrum focuses on how to scale product, Scaled Professional Scrum on how to scale teams, while the Scaled Agile Framework encompasses elements of both with an additional perspective of Portfolio Governance.

Large-Scale Scrum (LeSS)

Large-Scale Scrum addresses the issues of scale by focusing on the Product Owner role – defining how they should work with multiple teams towards a single shippable Product Increment.

The core is Scrum, with some events modified for coordination:

- Backlog Refinement is split into two: a light-touch Refinement with representatives from each team; followed by an in-depth Refinement team-by-team for all team members.

- The two parts of Sprint Planning are formally separated: in the first half, team representatives select Product Backlog Items for the coming Sprint; in the second half, each team then works independently to break these into Tasks as normal.

- Daily Scrums continue separately, with an additional **Town Hall** meeting – similar to the Scrum of Scrums (see page 162).

- The Sprint Review should include everyone involved, from all the teams, as well as stakeholders, partners, and third-parties.

- Sprint Retrospectives are still separate by team, although there is often an additional shared Retrospective afterwards.

To reflect the complexities of working with such a large Product Backlog and so many teams, there are also some roles changes:

- The Product Owners become **Area Product Owners**.

- On really complex products, there is a new role of **Chief Product Owner** responsible for the overall Product Backlog.

- This requires an additional pre-Sprint event for the Area Product Owners to coordinate how they manage the inevitable dependencies that will arise between the teams.

Scaled Professional Scrum

Scaled Professional Scrum helps organizations coordinate the work of 3-9 Scrum Teams working on the same product.

This builds out from a single team by establishing a **Nexus,** or broader framework, which gives a focus to the coordination and collaboration on dependencies between multiple teams.

A new team to integrate the work of Scrum Teams

To ensure the level of coordination and integration required, the Nexus has an **Integration Team**, to coordinate the work of the Scrum Teams. They also operate as a Scrum Team and should include all disciplines required to coordinate, integrate, and release Product Increments at the end of each Sprint.

A new high-level Sprint Backlog

Each Sprint, the teams pull work from the Product Backlog into a separate Sprint Backlog per team. To make this collective commitment transparent, these are collected together into a new higher level **Nexus Sprint Backlog**.

New Events

Some of the traditional Scrum events are replaced or amended:

- Sprints begin with a new **Nexus Sprint Planning**, where team representatives select Product Backlog Items for their respective teams – each team then separately meets to plan out its own Tasks, still interacting with other teams to highlight dependencies and coordinate their work.

- The **Nexus Daily Scrum** – equivalent to a Scrum of Scrums – for representatives of each team to jointly assess dependencies, with any action required taken back to the respective team.

- The **Nexus Sprint Review** brings all teams together to review the integrated Product Increment with the Product Owner.

- After each team's Sprint Retrospective, team representatives gather for the **Nexus Sprint Retrospective** to discuss shared challenges and identify actions for their teams.

Finally, with the complexities of planning and integrating the work of so many teams, there needs to be a higher investment in refining the Product Backlog – probably more than once per week.

...cont'd

Scaled Agile Framework (SAFe)

The **Scaled Agile Framework** applies lean and agile principles at all levels of project work: the portfolio, the program, and the delivery teams. SAFe is freely available, which has helped it to become the most frequently and widely implemented framework for operating agile projects at enterprise scale.

The key model in the framework is the big picture (simplified version below), which summarizes the key roles, processes, and artifacts, and how they interrelate. Note: the full diagram is available for free on the website – **www.scaledagileframework.com**

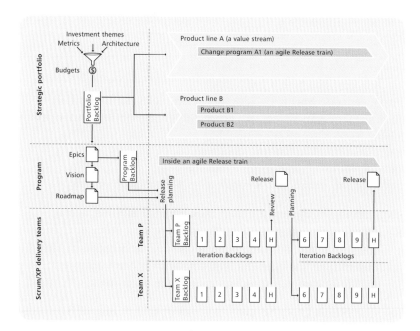

The core elements of SAFe

At the portfolio level, work is aligned to strategic themes through identified **Value Streams** (such as product lines) with a Backlog of business and architecture Epics that can span multiple Releases by being broken down into Features for Release Planning.

These Value Streams are implemented through work taking place within an **Agile Release Train,** which provides enough structure to orchestrate the build, test, and deployment of the product.

Agile Release Trains can house up to 15 teams, incrementally building Features which are released every five iterations or so.

Roles in SAFe

At the core of SAFe lie the **Scrum/XP teams**, with the same roles: Product Owner, Scrum Master, and up to nine team members.

At the program level, a **Product Manager** coordinates the Product Owners and is responsible for the program's Vision, Backlog and Roadmap. A **Release Train Engineer** coordinates the Scrum Masters and is responsible for program-level processes like Scrum of Scrums and Release Planning. They are supported by system, DevOps, and Release management teams and provide access to shared specialists across the program, such as UX, architecture, etc.

At the portfolio level, a **Portfolio Management Team** of senior executives looks after high-level financial and product Governance.

Practices in SAFe

At the team level, they follow the Scrum framework for team practices and Extreme Programming for code quality and technical principles (see page 105); which is why SAFe calls them Scrum/XP teams. Iterations at the team level follow the same principles as Sprints, progressively developing Stories until Features are complete enough for a Release.

SAFe promotes a continuous deployment approach, releasing products and new features to customers as soon as they are ready. However, SAFe does recognize that in complex operating environments, Releases often run on a longer cycle, and it recommends no longer than three months between Releases.

Each Release starts with Release Planning, runs through a number of development iterations, and typically ends with a hardening iteration, where the system is stabilized and readied for Release (see page 125). The Release is confirmed through a **Release Review**, and cross-team improvements are identified through a **Release Retrospective**. Backlog Refinement is continual.

The Portfolio Management Team use their agreed investment themes to funnel funding and work to program Backlogs for each respective program and its Agile Release Trains.

Finally, SAFe also recognizes that even organizations who have fully embraced feedback-driven development often have to run plan-driven programs too. To avoid duplication and redundancy in Governance, the SAFe model can operate them all in parallel.

Hot tip

Check out Project Program and Portfolio Management in easy steps for more information on this process.

Summary

- Scrum focuses on individual teams, and says nothing about how multiple teams work together.

- Large organizations typically have many teams across multiple locations, and legacy systems with which new products have to work.

- Any changes to legacy systems are typically managed through plan-driven projects, often causing significant delays to the feedback-driven teams who are dependent on those changes.

- With multiple teams working on the same Product Backlog, it is vital to plan and synchronize together – this means changing or combining some of the standard Scrum events.

- The Scrum of Scrums becomes a vital point of coordination for representatives of each team.

- Deploying product at scale is even more challenging than for a single team. However, it is vital to ensure the teams can integrate and orchestrate their work seamlessly.

- To cope with scaling feedback-driven product development, Governance has to become leaner or it will fail.

- Senior leadership have to get tougher with their portfolio, limiting the number of in-flight projects, being quicker to cancel lower-return projects in favor of higher priorities, and always looking to release value early where possible.

- Organizations benefit from taking a longer-term product management perspective rather than a short-term project one.

- Several frameworks have emerged that help address aspects of this, but none of them address every aspect of concern.

- Large-Scale Scrum maintains a product management focus across potentially massively scaled projects.

- Scaled Professional Scrum provides a way of coordinating work across up to nine teams through the Nexus.

- The Scaled Agile Framework addresses portfolio and program concerns, as well as how to coordinate the work of multiple teams, including those on plan-driven programs.

11 The Scrum reference

Scrum is one of the most popular agile frameworks for product development.

This chapter is a quick reference to the Scrum framework with its roles, events, artifacts, and rules.

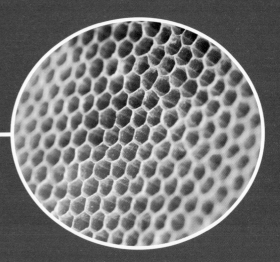

The Scrum framework

This chapter is a quick reference for the Scrum framework. It summarizes and reprises the information provided throughout the rest of this book:

- Chapter One explains the business drivers for adopting a feedback-driven product development framework like Scrum.

- Chapters Two through to Nine take you step-by-step from forming your first Scrum Team and creating a Product Vision, to delivering the product to market and reflecting how to get better at doing that.

- Chapter Ten explores how organizations can scale up from their first team to cope with multiple teams working across multiple products.

The framework

The framework on which Scrum is based is a small set of loosely defined rules. These rules describe the responsibilities, timings, and deliverables that enable feedback-driven product development. These combine iterative design, incremental development, self-organizing teams, and continual improvement.

Being a framework, rather than a prescribed methodology of practices, means that organizations can use a number of techniques to discover, design, and build their products – such as Extreme Programming (see page 105) and UX design (see page 56) – so long as they are complementary to Scrum.

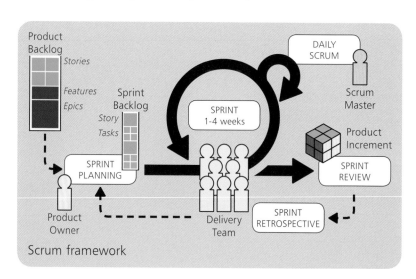

Scrum framework

The Scrum framework consists of the Scrum Team (and the roles within it), the events that take place, the artifacts used and produced, and the rules that define how these all interact:

The Scrum Team

There are three key roles within the team:

- **Product Owner**: responsible for the business value of the product, defining why and selecting what gets done.

- **Delivery Team**: a self-organizing group of programmers, testers, analysts, etc. – responsible for deciding how the work gets done and completing it – also known as the *Development Team*.

- **Scrum Master**: ensures that the team is motivated, productive, and applying their agreed principles and practices.

Scrum events

There are five events central to the Scrum framework:

- **Sprint**: the time-box (normally two weeks) within which all work and other events take place.

- **Sprint Planning**: the team and Product Owner agree what Features to do in a Sprint, then define the Tasks required.

- **Daily Scrum**: the team plan the work for that day, and based on progress and Impediments, re-plan the rest of the Sprint.

- **Sprint Review**: the team demonstrate their progress to their stakeholders and gather their feedback.

- **Sprint Retrospective**: the team looks back at how the last Sprint went and agree possible team improvement actions.

Scrum artifacts

There are three core Scrum artifacts:

- **Product Backlog**: the prioritized requirements list of desired product Features and other required work.

- **Sprint Backlog**: a sub-set of work from the Product Backlog that the team agrees to complete in a Sprint, with Tasks.

- **Product Increment**: the Features of the product the team has built in a Sprint, on top of product Features already released.

Scrum foundations

Product development is a creative process, in which team members collaborate in building solutions to complex problems, and obtaining feedback that enables them to learn and improve.

Creating a framework to support this creativity has to be based on loose constraints with clear expectations and measurements. This is suited to an experiential learning cycle. Knowledge and understanding come from planning something, doing it, reviewing how well it went, and then adapting the process for the next cycle.

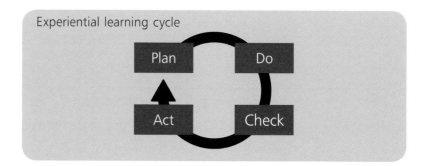

Experiential learning cycle

As an iterative process, Scrum fits this model at three levels:

- At the daily work level these four stages equate to planning at the Daily Scrum, working on selected tasks, then reviewing and drawing conclusions in the following Daily Scrum.

- At the Sprint level, the four stages equate to Sprint Planning, working through the Sprint Backlog, followed by the Sprint Review and the Sprint Retrospective.

- Although not formally part of Scrum, there is also a higher level of planning, execution, and feedback based on the Release cycle (covered in Chapters Six, Seven, and Eight).

Empirical Process Control
To be confident that they are developing the right functionality in the right way, teams need an evidence-based approach that seeks feedback as often as possible.

To support this, Scrum is founded on **Empirical Process Control**. Rather than approaching a problem with a grand theory or set of assumptions, Empirical Process Control is based on the principles of **Transparency**, **Inspection**, and **Adaptation**.

Transparency

In Scrum, the team's progress and the process they are following is visible on their Scrum Board. The team also define and reference a Definition of Done (see page 88) to establish a common understanding of standards for development and quality assurance.

Inspection

In Scrum, the team's progress and artifacts are inspected frequently as they work. To avoid this becoming an Impediment, it should either be undertaken by experienced practitioners in the team or be based on metrics where applicable.

Adaptation

Whenever the results of an inspection indicate that the process or artifact has deviated outside of tolerance levels, such that the Product Increment would be not be accepted, adjustments need to be made to the product or to the process being followed.

Any adjustment has to be made as close as possible to when the deviation is discovered, to reduce the risk of additional problems.

Points of Inspection and Adaptation

Although teams should inspect and adapt whenever required, there are points in Scrum that provide a formal opportunity:

- The team collaborates during Backlog Refinement and Sprint Planning to ensure that work is well enough defined.

- While work is underway, code reviews are used to inspect the internal quality, while a range of manual and automated tests will determine if the product meets the Acceptance Criteria.

- Each day in the Daily Scrum, the team review their progress, highlight any Impediments, and consider what action to take.

- As the team completes their work, the Product Owner will inspect it and confirm that everything has been Done or whether further work is required.

- At the end of the Sprint, the team elicit feedback from their stakeholders in the Sprint Review.

- Finally, in the Sprint Retrospective, the team review their experience of the Sprint to determine if they need to change the way they are working.

Scrum roles

The Scrum Team consists of the Delivery Team working with the Product Owner, facilitated by the Scrum Master.

Product Owner
The Product Owner maximizes the value of their product, by working with the Delivery Team to:

- Define and prioritize items on the Product Backlog.

- Ensure they understand what is required.

The Product Owner's responsibilities are explored throughout this book, especially Chapters Three to Five, covering Product Discovery.

The Delivery Team
The Delivery Team delivers a potentially shippable Product Increment each Sprint, by working with the Product Owner to:

- Understand the Product Backlog and get it ready for work.

- Determine the technical solution that meets organizational constraints, Acceptance Criteria, and delivers value.

- Collaborate across all disciplines to complete work in a priority order that reduces risk and achieves the Sprint goal.

The team's responsibilities are described throughout this book, especially in Chapters Six to Eight, covering product Delivery.

Scrum Master
The Scrum Master facilitates the work, by working with the Delivery Team and Product Owner to:

- Coach them in Scrum and technical practices.

- Help the team to solve Impediments as they arise.

- Hold the team accountable for their commitments.

The Scrum Master's responsibilities are explained throughout this book, especially in Chapters Nine and Ten.

Ancillary roles
There are also ancillary roles, such as stakeholders (customers or vendors) and managers (project or line) who, while not part of the team, are important to its success. These ancillary roles are further explored in Chapter Two.

The Delivery Team is also known as the *Development Team*.

Scrum events

There are five time-boxed events central to the Scrum framework.

Sprint
The time-box (normally of two weeks) within which all work and events take place. Anything that takes place outside of the Sprint is not formally regarded as part of the Scrum framework.

Sprint Planning
A session at the beginning of each Sprint in which the team agrees with the Product Owner what functionality they will build in the upcoming Sprint. The team also defines the tasks required to complete that functionality. Covered in Chapter Six.

Daily Scrum
A 15-minute session, once per day, where the team considers their progress in order to plan the work for that day, and raise any Impediments that require resolution or escalation. Covered in Chapter Seven.

Sprint Review
A session at the end of each Sprint in which the team shows what progress they have made to their stakeholders, and gathers feedback. Based on that feedback, there may be additional items for the Product Backlog. Covered in Chapter Eight.

Sprint Retrospective
A session at the end of each Sprint in which the team looks back at their productivity, morale, and behavior over the last Sprint. They agree how to maintain positive outcomes and identify possible team improvement actions. Covered in Chapter Nine.

Non-core events
In addition to these core Scrum events, many teams also plan time for the following events:

- **Discovery workshops**: where key stakeholders work with the Product Owner to define the product (see Chapter Three).

- **Backlog Refinement**: in which members of the team work with the Product Owner to prepare the Product Backlog, so that it is ready for Sprint Planning (see Chapter Four).

- **Release Planning**: where the team commit to the Features they plan to build for the next three months (see Chapter Five).

Scrum artifacts

There are three core Scrum artifacts.

Product Backlog
The register of all required work, including: Epics, Features, Stories, Bugs, Defects, Spikes, and team improvements. These items are collectively referred to as Product Backlog Items (PBI).

The Product Owner ensures that PBIs are well-formed and forecasts the Business Value, while the team assesses the size. Combining these two perspectives creates an order of work that first focuses on Features that will have the greatest impact in the shortest time. This is described in Chapter Five.

Sprint Backlog
The Sprint Backlog is a subset of PBIs and associated Tasks, agreed for one Sprint. As part of Sprint Planning, the Product Owner presents the most important PBIs for the team to ensure they understand what is required, and are confident can be completed in a single Sprint. Those PBIs and Tasks agreed are added to the Sprint Backlog. This is explained in Chapter Six.

Product Increment
The mission for a team is to progressively add functionality to the product each Sprint, so that the product grows towards completion. This is usually a combination of new Features, modifications to existing functionality, and improvements to quality that have been integrated with all previous work. Building the Product Increment is covered in Chapter Seven.

At the end of each Sprint, the Product Increment that has been built should be potentially shippable. That is, when released to customers it would be usable and generate some value. The Product Owner decides when to release, and often waits to integrate Product Increments from several Sprints before releasing. Delivering the Product Increments is covered in Chapter Eight.

Additional artifacts
In addition to the core Scrum artifacts, teams often find additional artifacts useful, such as: a Scrum Board, a Sprint Burn-Down Chart, a Release Burn-Up Chart, and a Risk Board.

Both the core and the additional artifacts are discussed in context throughout the book.

The rules of Scrum

The following rules help the roles, events, and artifacts operate:

General Rules of Scrum

- Every Sprint is of the same duration; usually two weeks.

- Every Sprint has time set aside for Scrum events, time-boxed as follows for the typical two-week Sprint:

  - Sprint Planning – four hours

  - Daily Scrum – 15 minutes

  - Sprint Review – two hours

  - Sprint Retrospectives – 90 minutes

- There are no breaks between Sprints.

- The goal is to produce a potentially shippable Product Increment by the end of every Sprint.

- Once the Sprint has started, no change is permitted that would affect the Sprint goal – except for the decision to cancel it.

- Product Backlog Items are sized by the team who will implement them.

- The Daily Scrum occurs every day in the same place at the same time, unless it clashes with another critical Scrum event.

- At the Daily Scrum, team members discuss only what they have progressed with, and what is blocking progress.

- All stakeholders are invited to attend the Sprint Review.

- A Scrum Team includes only the Product Owner, Scrum Master, and Delivery Team members.

- A Delivery Team has between three and nine people.

- Team membership cannot be changed during the Sprint.

Canceling a Sprint

A Sprint may be canceled – at the discretion of the Product Owner – if the Sprint goal has become obsolete. All completed work should be reviewed, and if reusable, accepted. Anything left undone is moved back onto the Product Backlog or discarded.

The origins of Scrum

Combining the early thinking around iterative design and incremental development (see Chapter One), two development leaders, Ken Schwaber and Jeff Sutherland, developed a feedback-driven framework for product development they called **Scrum**. They jointly presented this early framework at a 1995 software development conference in Austin, Texas.

Over the following years, their thinking evolved as they collaborated on defining the framework and rules for Scrum. The complete framework was first fully defined in the book *Agile Software Development with Scrum* by Ken Schwaber and Mike Beedle.

Scrum certification and ongoing development
There are two recognized paths to accreditation for Product Owners, Scrum Masters, and Developers:

- **Scrum Alliance** oversees the Certified Scrum programs.

- **Scrum.org** manages the Professional Scrum accreditations.

Together, Schwaber and Sutherland continue to develop the Scrum framework, which they make available for free through their Scrum Guide website – **www.scrumguides.org**

The Agile Manifesto
In 2001, Schwaber and Sutherland met with 15 other representatives of lightweight software development methods. They discussed alternatives to plan-driven approaches and established a common understanding, which they published:

Manifesto for Agile Software Development

We are uncovering better ways of developing software by doing it and helping others do it. Through this work we have come to value:

Individuals and interactions over processes and tools

Working software over comprehensive documentation

Customer collaboration over contract negotiation

Responding to change over following a plan

That is, while there is value in the items on the right, we value the items on the left more.

The Manifesto principles

The Agile Manifesto is underpinned by these 12 principles:

1   **Customer satisfaction**: by the early and continual delivery of valuable software

2   **Changing requirements**: are welcomed, even late in the development process

3   **Frequent delivery**: of working software, from every couple of weeks to every couple of months

4   **Close cooperation**: business people and team members must work together daily throughout the project

5   **Motivate individuals**: by giving them the support they need and trusting them to get the job done

6   **Face-to-face conversation**: the most efficient and effective method of conveying information in a Delivery Team

7   **Working software**: delivery of working software is the principle measure of progress

8   **Sustainable development**: so sponsors, team members, and stakeholders can maintain a constant pace indefinitely

9   **Technical excellence**: through continuous attention to technical excellence and good design

10   **Simplicity**: by keeping things simple the amount of work that has to be done is minimized

11   **Self-organizing teams**: allow the best architectures, requirements and designs to emerge

12   **Regular adaptation**: the team reflects on how to become more effective and adjusts its behavior accordingly

Summary

- Scrum provides a framework (the team, events, artifacts and rules) within which people can address complex problems.

- Scrum is based on experiential learning that goes through a cycle of planning, executing, reviewing, and concluding.

- The Scrum Team consists of the Product Owner, the Delivery Team and the Scrum Master.

- The optimum size for the Delivery Team is between five and nine people (not counting the Product Owner and Scrum Master).

- The Scrum Master's role is to facilitate the team's work, deal with any Impediments, and ensure the correct processes are being followed.

- Sprints typically last two weeks, and start with Sprint Planning, followed by Daily Scrums, and end with a Sprint Review and Sprint Retrospective.

- Sprint Planning takes place in a time-boxed meeting in which the Delivery Team agrees with the Product Owner what they can include in the Sprint Backlog, and what Tasks are needed to complete them.

- The Daily Scrum lasts 15 minutes in which each team member says what they have just completed, what they plan to do next, and whether there are any Impediments.

- The Sprint Review inspects the Product Increment and agrees any changes required to the Product Backlog.

- The Sprint Retrospective gives the team the chance to look back at the Sprint and develop a plan for implementing any team improvements.

- The Product Backlog is the sequenced list of all known requirements for the product.

- The Sprint Backlog is the work to be carried out in the Sprint and the plan for how it will be done.

- Progress monitoring is done through estimating the work still to be actioned, and plotting this against the planned Velocity.

Index

G

H

I

J

K

L

M

T

U

V

W